"Thirty-five years ago, Richard Foster introduced a generation to the spiritual disciplines. Now his son introduces another generation to both the glories and the frustrations of seeking to practice them—to master and be mastered by the craft and art of the spiritual life. This is a book of honesty and hope."

—**John Ortberg,** senior pastor of Menlo Park
Presbyterian Church; author of *Soul Keeping*

"I learned a new word recently: *self-implication.* It was used by a friend writing on participation in the Christian life in which she was concerned not just with being accurate with the biblical and theological content but with being herself implicated in the narration. This is what Nathan Foster has done—written about the Christian life not impersonally and objectively but as a participant. Read this book and find yourself a new companion as you follow Jesus."

—**Eugene H. Peterson,** professor emeritus
of spiritual theology, Regent College

"Nathan Foster's *The Making of an Ordinary Saint* breathes fresh life into the same ancient practices his father resuscitated for millions of ordinary people almost forty years ago. His conversational style and unvarnished transparency make his living experiment inviting for other ordinary saints in the making."

—**Gary W. Moon,** executive director of the Martin Institute and
Dallas Willard Center, Westmont College;
author of *Apprenticeship with Jesus*

"Delightful . . . simply delightful. Nathan's reflections on the spiritual disciplines are honest, fresh, and insightful. Read and be blessed."

—**Ruth Haley Barton,** founder, Transforming Center;
author of *Strengthening the Soul of Your Leadership*
and *Sacred Rhythms*

"Nathan has a unique voice so badly needed today. He is a storyteller whose raw honesty disarms the reader and allows us to join him, without fear of judgment, on a journey toward an imperfect sainthood. As a longtime practitioner of his father's classic, *Celebration of Discipline*, I found this book to be a fresh retelling of the same teachings through a modern narrative. Nathan zeroes in on the internal issues that each of the disciplines unearth and in doing so allows me to see the value of these ancient practices in a new light. The highest endorsement I can offer is this: just like his father's book did for me thirty years ago, I want, really want, to practice these disciplines. That was Richard's genius; it has passed on to his son."

—**James Bryan Smith**, associate professor of religion, Friends University; executive director of the Apprentice Institute; author of The Apprentice Series

"Nathan shows us that spiritual disciplines are not rigid things to do but invitational experiments, guiding songs, and adventurous romps with God to explore a life of trust. Let's try them out!"

—**Jan Johnson**, author of *Spiritual Disciplines Companion* and *Invitation to the Jesus Life*

"Smart, informative, invitational, honest, helpful. Those are the words that came to mind as I finished Nathan Foster's *The Making of an Ordinary Saint*. With no small assist from reflections by his father, Foster's book opens the celebration of the disciplines to a whole new generation. This book is at times raw but always loving as Foster tells of his journey of spiritual deepening in the midst of everyday life. You must read this book!"

—**J. Brent Bill**, Quaker minister; retreat leader; photographer; author of *Sacred Compass: The Way of Spiritual Discernment*

"Nathan Foster is living with an ache, a space that only God can fill. His book lets us share slow, sometimes painful, grace-filled movements of the Spirit as he explores ancient disciplines and identifies his own awkward resistance to God's transforming love. He finds worlds of meaning in practical and biblical metaphors: drafting (a biking term) becomes a word for community-building, slavery (as St. Paul unfolds it) a way to surrender fully to God's will. What an honest, loving, joyful gift."

—**Emilie Griffin**, author of *Doors into Prayer: An Invitation* and co-editor with Richard J. Foster of *Spiritual Classics*

"Nathan Foster has written a deeply personal and honest story about his own life with God. In doing so, he beckons us to trust that in the midst of our daily life, we too can follow Jesus. With *The Making of an Ordinary Saint*, Nathan captures the essence of how to go about living in the freedom of God's unbridled goodness, strength, and care. If you are ready to experience the God who loves you as you are, not as you should be, this is the book for you!"

—**Fil Anderson**, author of *Running on Empty* and *Breaking the Rules*

THE MAKING OF AN ORDINARY SAINT

My Journey from Frustration to Joy
with the Spiritual Disciplines

NATHAN FOSTER

BakerBooks
a division of Baker Publishing Group
Grand Rapids, Michigan

© 2014 by Nathan Foster

Published by Baker Books
a division of Baker Publishing Group
P.O. Box 6287, Grand Rapids, MI 49516-6287
www.bakerbooks.com

Printed in the United States of America

Library of Congress Cataloging-in-Publication Data
Foster, Nathan.
    The making of an ordinary saint : my journey from frustration to joy with the spiritual disciplines / Nathan Foster.
        pages cm
    Includes bibliographical references.
    ISBN 978-0-8010-1464-2 (pbk.)
    1. Spiritual life--Christianity. 2. Spiritual biography. I. Title.
BV4501.3.F677 2014
248.4'6--dc23   2014017529

Unless otherwise indicated, Scripture quotations are from the New Revised Standard Version of the Bible, copyright © 1989, by the Division of Christian Education of the National Council of the Churches of Christ in the United States of America. Used by permission. All rights reserved.

Scripture quotations labeled KJV are from the King James Version of the Bible.

Scripture quotations labeled Message are from *The Message* by Eugene H. Peterson, copyright © 1993, 1994, 1995, 2000, 2001, 2002. Used by permission of NavPress Publishing Group. All rights reserved.

Scripture quotations labeled NIV are from the Holy Bible, New International Version®. NIV®. Copyright © 1973, 1978, 1984, 2011 by Biblica, Inc.™ Used by permission of Zondervan. All rights reserved worldwide. www.zondervan.com

The reflections on the disciplines were contributed by Richard J. Foster. The biographical portraits at the end of each chapter were contributed by Robbie Bolton. Used by permission.

The author is represented by Creative Trust, Inc., Literary Division, 5141 Virginia Way, Suite 320, Brentwood, TN 37027, www.creativetrust.com.

15   16   17   18   19   20   21   8   7   6   5   4   3   2

To Christy,

for carrying me when I could no longer walk.

Contents

Contents

Foreword

Throughout Christian history (and even before), there has been a great conversation about the growth of the soul. How is human character formed and transformed? Is it possible for us to grow in virtue? Can we genuinely develop the moral character of Jesus so that we do indeed think God's thoughts after him? If so, how exactly does this happen? How should we best understand the developmental nature of Christian spirituality? Is it possible to rightly order our love for God in such a way that we can actually make progress forward in the spiritual life? These questions—and a thousand others like them—have been studied and discussed and debated all through the Christian centuries. In one form or another, these matters have been a continuing theme in all the devotional classics.

Think of the writings of Evagrius Ponticus on the "deadly thoughts" and the "godly virtues"—our discussions today about "the seven deadly sins" draw directly from his writings. Or think of Origen of Alexandria and his forty-two stages of the soul's journey. Or consider Teresa of Avila and her *Interior Castle*, or Saint John of the Cross and his *Dark Night of the Soul*. The list could go on for a long time indeed.

I say all of this to underscore the fact that we have a long and respected tradition about how the human personality grows in virtue and in the fruit of the Spirit: love, joy, peace, patience, kindness, goodness, faithfulness, gentleness, and self-control. With *The Making of an Ordinary Saint*, Nathan Foster steps directly into the mainstream of this tradition.

Nathan makes three important contributions to the great conversation about the growth of the soul. First, his insights come to us in narrative form. The vast majority of writings on these themes are given to us in didactic form. Of course, direct teaching is not a wrong approach and can often be quite helpful. Much of my own writings are didactic in character. But Nathan writes to us on the slant, if you will. He tells us stories, most importantly his own story. He leads us on the journey of how he began growing in grace and what his journey can teach us about a continuing with-God kind of life. This stands in the tradition of Augustine of Hippo and his *Confessions*, of Julian of Norwich and her *Showings*, of John Woolman and his *Journal*. Closer to our own day, I think of Thomas Merton and his *Seven Storey Mountain* and Frank Laubach and his *Letters by a Modern Mystic*. A narrative approach adds depth and variety to the great conversation about the growth of the soul.

Second, Nathan shares with us out of the context of ordinary life. Frankly, many of the writings we have about the growth of the soul have grown out of monastic settings. Now, these settings have substantial advantages and have given us a wealth of wisdom. But they also have considerable drawbacks. Perhaps the most pointed drawback was famously expressed by the caustic comment of John Milton, "I cannot praise a fugitive and cloistered virtue." You see, it is one thing to experience progress in moral virtue when everything in our day is ordered around the hours of prayer and where there is an absence of many of life's everyday frustrations. It is quite another to learn to "pray without ceasing" in the midst of an overbearing boss, children clamoring for our attention, dishes piling up in the sink, and a shortage of money to pay the heating bill.

Nathan has much to teach us here. He engages the Christian spiritual disciplines smack in the midst of all the frustrations you and I must face in our daily lives. He never holds back from sharing with us the many difficulties and frustrations of his efforts. Indeed, the subtitle to his book is quite telling: "My Journey from Frustration to Joy with the Spiritual Disciplines."

This leads to a third contribution, which in some ways is the most significant of all. In Nathan's efforts to describe for us the struggles of an ordinary person in ordinary circumstances, he is careful to share with us the full range of human emotion: anger, joy, fear, ecstasy, exasperation, delight, agony, and more. You see, in religious circles (as in all circles, I suppose), it is so tempting for us to share only the mountaintop victories, the glorious healings, the astonishing triumphs of the human spirit. We draw back or perhaps ignore our less than stellar moments or even outright failures in our practice of the spiritual disciplines. And consequently, how elusive is our progress into Christlikeness, into sanctification of life. Or, conversely, we will swing to the other extreme and simply glory in our wretchedness, a kind of gutter-to-the-cross saga.

Here Nathan brings us into genuine balance. He never shies away from plunging us into the painfulness of shortcomings, but he also helps us experience with joy the steps forward into Christlikeness. The full range of emotions is ours as we walk with Nathan in his multi-year experimentations with the spiritual disciplines.

With *The Making of an Ordinary Saint*, Nathan Foster has made a valuable contribution to the great conversation about the growth of the soul. Get this book. Read this book. Allow this book to lead you into your own experiences with the classical disciplines of the spiritual life.

Richard J. Foster

Introduction

Beginnings

The truth is that everyone is bored, and devotes himself to cultivating habits.

Albert Camus[1]

In 1978, my father, Richard J. Foster, wrote *Celebration of Discipline*.[2] The book was well received; it has sold some two million copies in English and has been translated into twenty-five other languages.[3] It continues to be taught in multiple settings from seminaries and universities to Sunday schools and home study groups. It is beginning to be referenced in history books for its influence on Christianity. Many have noted that my dad's work helped launch a movement toward what we know today as spiritual formation.

My father is now retired, and his formal public life is ending. As he comes to this end, he feels discouraged. "It's almost as if spiritual formation is just another fad in Western Christianity," he told me. "The disciplines aren't merely pious exercises for the devout. People don't seem to understand the 'big picture' of how the disciplines are a means of grace to transform the human personality."

I wonder about that "big picture."

I wonder what spiritual formation is all about.

Dad said he wrote *Celebration of Discipline* for all those who are disillusioned with the superficialities of modern culture.

I'm disillusioned—not just with the shallowness of our culture but with life in general. I spend more time lost with the question "Is this all there is to life?" than I care to admit.

I'm in my midthirties, and for the first time I'm starting to understand some of the midlife issues people often struggle with. Recently, my older brother joined the Air Force and was deployed to Iraq. Working in a medical unit there, my brother, who once had a bumper sticker that read "Who would Jesus bomb?" now talks about guns and bomber planes, carelessly throwing around terms I don't understand like *theater of war* and *AFSC*. I have to give him credit for being far more creative in his midlife crisis than the traditional manner of buying a red convertible and having an affair. I think mentioning this sort of offended him, as did my sloppy salute and "Aye, aye, Captain!" I guess he's not that type of captain.

While I'm not interested in either midlife crisis option, and my work teaching at a university is extremely meaningful, I feel lost in this frustration that I spend my days feeling overwhelmed by doing things that don't really matter to me. I'm a little embarrassed to admit it, but my silly hobbies mean a whole lot more to me than the other ways I spend my time. I guess I'm looking for a new quest, new dragons to slay, much like my brother.

It feels unfair and a little cliché to say, but I'm also disillusioned with the church. I get why males in my generation are leaving in droves. There are many good things about organized religion that I find valuable: it helps me connect with others, it gives me a place to serve, and my kids seem to like it. But I have next to no expectation of church facilitating a space for me to connect with God. So often it seems like just another noisy, busy activity that fills my schedule. I'm left living with an ache, an intuitive longing for a deeper spiritual connection.

I don't know what to do with that, but a new program, sermon series, study, or service project, as good and well intended as it may be, doesn't seem to change much. I'm not critical or angry about this; it is what it is.

I find I think a lot about life, death, and my place in this mysterious venture we call human existence. In recent years, I've found myself nostalgically drawn to reading, watching, and visiting anything historical. With childlike imagination I've tiptoed through history looking for my place among the tombs of my genetic past. When visiting an old British castle or Native American reservation, a hush overtakes me. I caress the walls and study the pictures, desperately searching for connection. I re-create stories and imagine I've finally discovered the home of my people, like a lost explorer returning to an empty village.

I don't know what to do with the echoing memories of human history. I listen and try to learn. When I pay homage to the past, I find meaning and the courage to show up for life. I often think of my loved ones who have passed away and wonder if I carry the hopes and dreams they had for me. As odd as it may sound, I want them to be proud of me.

And so this was the proverbial soup that spawned this project. It started with a scenario from my overly dramatic imagination. I was an old man gingerly navigating a dusty and flower-speckled Colorado canyon trail, relying heavily on a tattered, hand-carved stick, my wrinkled and weathered frame ambling along. This was my dad's canyon. For the last half of his life he had come here often. His thoughts and prayers were locked in these walls; this was his old castle, his vacant farmhouse. In my daydream, I was there to honor his passing. Resting on the bench I had donated to the state park to place in his memory, I cracked open a faded red book my father had written when I was four years old. I imagined I was at the end of a yearlong process of diligently studying and experimenting with the twelve ancient spiritual practices found in that book. It was a project to say good-bye to him, to process my grief.

And there it was: my new challenge lay before me. What if I spent an entire year intentionally and intensely working on my spiritual life, following the instruction from one of my father's books? The project would be to creatively and intentionally work with what he had outlined in his book *Celebration of Discipline* as twelve historic practices of the Christian faith: submission, fasting, study, solitude, meditation, confession, simplicity, service, prayer, guidance, worship, and the one I personally dreaded the most—celebration.

Funny, I had been almost giddy about this idea. It never occurred to me that I might be embarking on something terribly boring and potentially painful. I had a project, something to do with my angst and lost hope for life. I was beginning a journey into modern-day "monkhood," though of course without the robes or celibacy. My one-year experiment would eventually turn into four.

The concept of the spiritual disciplines is really quite simple: we do the practices that Jesus did. Over time these practices become habitual, thus enabling us to respond to life in a way more like Jesus would if he were to live our life. As we submit our will to spiritual practices, God's grace brings forth character transformation. This seems to be the dominant means God uses to bring about change in our lives. Christian spiritual formation is the process of becoming people formed into the likeness of Christ's character. If I want to respond to life with love, joy, peace, forbearance, kindness, goodness, faithfulness, gentleness, and self-control, I can't just force or fake it. When someone cuts me off in traffic, I quickly learn the quality of my spiritual habits. So if I practice living like Jesus did, then God takes my little effort and begins to form within me a person who naturally responds to life well. This is what the old writers called being a "well-established person."

The most frequently cited metaphor for understanding the point and power of the disciplines is that of athletes in training. Being able to perform athletic feats is only possible because of the hours upon hours of specialized preparation. After shooting the game-winning shot in the 1993 NBA finals, John Paxson said, "I just caught the ball and shot it as I have my whole life. I've been playing basketball since I was eight years old, and I've shot like that in my driveway hundreds of thousands of times. It was just reaction."[4]

In his book *Outliers*, Malcolm Gladwell challenges the commonly held belief that luck has to do with success.[5] He sets forth the idea that practice—ten thousand hours of practice, to be precise—is what brings about expertise in any realm. The common denominator from professional athletes to Bill Gates to the Beatles is that they all practiced intensely at their craft before they rose to the public's attention. I don't know about praying for ten thousand hours, but it's a place to start.

"Nate, it's a little like this," my dad would say. "I can put a basketball in the hoop given enough tries, but I can't do it when it needs to be done. Look at the top stars who are able to score in clutch time in games. That's only because they have trained for years."

"So maybe one way to quit being selfish and yelling at my kids is to spend more time with the disciplines? Would it then become a habit to respond to life with more patience and self-control?" I asked.

"Yeah, Nate, you're on the right track."

Apparently in the first century AD when Paul said to "train unto righteousness,"[6] this was something they understood in their culture. In his day the success of athletes was seen as more of a product of training than of natural ability.

Practice develops into habit, for better or, unfortunately, for worse. For example, if we continually practice poor nutrition, we become very good at eating things that are bad for us. Here is another way to look at the topic: virtue is good habits we can rely upon to make our lives work well; vice is destructive habits we can rely upon to destroy our lives. Both are habits.

It's hard to remember that seeing the results from our habits takes time. Lots of time. We don't gain fifty pounds or learn to smoke two packs a day overnight. Neither do we suddenly quit being a self-centered egomaniac who micromanages others. Growing fruit takes time. In our society, we want instant results. We have no interest in taking two years to get into shape or thirty years to succeed. Much like it takes years of practice for a person to play Mozart's Requiem well, we can't be trapped into thinking spiritual formation will happen in forty days or even forty months. This work, this process, involves more like forty years.

Unfortunately, our religious culture expects people to automatically be well established when they come into the faith. As a result, good people with good intentions who desperately want to do the right thing end up faking the spiritual life, pretending they have things together, or just hiding who they really are all because they either don't have the tools or haven't put in the years. Rather than our churches becoming places where people can be open and vulnerable about their journeys, where people work toward spiritual growth, they so often become some of the most dishonest and disingenuous of gatherings.

I can still hear my dad whisper with excitement, "Nate, can't you see? The end result of practicing the disciplines is actually *joy!*"

The idea of becoming spiritually formed made sense, but the joy part was completely lost on me. Fasting and confession seemed too serious, saintly, and monastic to be joyful. Joy is for children, not adults, and certainly not men. Joy is roller coasters, wanderlust, and Santa Claus, not prayer and solitude.

So instead of joining the military or buying a red convertible, I decided to go saint.

But before I launched into my journey, something strange happened that began a profound shift in the way I looked at the disciplines.

It all started with a bike ride.

Understanding
Submission

Submission is the spiritual discipline that frees us from the everlasting burden of always needing to get our own way. In submission we are learning to hold things lightly. We are also learning to diligently watch over the spirit in which we hold others—honoring them, preferring them, loving them.

Submission is not age or gender specific. We are all—men and women, girls and boys—learning to follow the wise counsel of the apostle Paul to "be subject to one another out of reverence for Christ."[1] We—each and every one of us regardless of our position or station in life—are to engage in mutual subordination out of reverence for Christ.

The touchstone for the Christian understanding of submission is Jesus's astonishing statement, "If any want to become my followers, let them deny themselves and take up their cross and follow me."[2] This call of Jesus to "self-denial" is simply a way of coming to understand that we do not have to have our own way. It has nothing to do with self-contempt or self-hatred. It does not mean the loss of our identity or our individuality. It means quite simply the freedom to give way to others. It means to hold the interests of others above our own. It means freedom from self-pity and self-absorption.

Indeed, self-denial is the only true path to self-fulfillment. To save our life is to lose it; to lose our life for Christ's sake is to save it (see Mark 8:35). This strange paradox of discovering fulfillment through self-denial is wonderfully expressed in the poetic words of George Matheson:

> Make me a captive, Lord,
>   And then I shall be free;
> Force me to render up my sword,
>   And I shall conqueror be.
> I sink in life's alarms
>   When by myself I stand;
> Imprison me within Thine arms,
>   And strong shall be my hand.[3]

The foremost symbol of submission is the cross. "And being found in human form, [Jesus] humbled himself and became obedient to the point of death—even death on a cross."[4] Now, it was not just a "cross death" that Jesus experienced but a daily "cross life" of submission and service. And we are called to this constant, everyday "cross life" of submission and service.

All the spiritual disciplines have the potential to become destructive if misused, but submission is especially susceptible to this problem. As a result, we need to be clear regarding its limits. The limits of the discipline of submission are at the points at which it becomes destructive. It then becomes a denial of the law of love as taught by Jesus and is an affront to genuine Christian submission. These limits are not always easy to define. Often we are forced to deal with complicated issues simply because human relationships are complicated. But deal with them we must. And we have the assurance that the Holy Spirit will be with us to guide us through the discernment process.

Richard J. Foster

1

Submission

Submitting to the Will
of Wind and Children

Upon having his monastery invaded by Chinese soldiers and a gun pointed in his face, the Tibetan monk remained calm, continuing his prayers. The soldier angrily shouted, "Don't you realize I have the power to kill you?" Undeterred in his prayers, the monk replied, "Don't you realize I have the power to let you?"

For two days I cut through twenty-mile-per-hour winds on a bicycle for two hundred twenty-four miles across rural Ohio. I can't believe I paid money to endure twenty hours of torture with three thousand other lunatics. Never again.

I won't belabor the details of the night before the ride and the five hours of sleep I had in a police parking lot while lightning and rain raged outside my minivan, or the frustration of the night after the first day of riding when I tried to sleep on a high school gym floor to the accompaniment of thirty chronic snorers, or the mystery of the gym lights surprisingly set ablaze at 5:00 a.m. What I want to talk about is simply the ride.

When I signed up for this adventure, my only expectation was to finish without excruciating pain. It was early spring, and my winter legs were hardly prepared for a ride of this length. The idea that I would have to battle such wind never crossed my mind when I left home for this journey. After only thirty minutes of wrestling my invisible opponent, my unrelenting pride was the only thing that kept me from calling my wife and begging her to come rescue me!

I was completely spent. Mother Nature brooded from every direction, wobbling my flimsy cycle back and forth. The prospect of slugging through over a hundred miles of her frigid rage struck me with profound terror. My only hope lay in finding a group to ride with.

Drafting is when two or more cyclists ride inches behind each other, creating a sort of wind tunnel. It's as exhilarating as it is nerve-wracking riding just inches from a stranger's tire at twenty-plus mph. But some say that when you follow closely behind another rider, you can reduce your workload by up to 30 percent. On a ride like that day's, I was sure to encounter a multitude of herds huddled together, pedaling in unison in what is known as a paceline.

I usually avoid drafting; I don't care to exchange the scenery of a backcountry ride for a prolonged view of someone's spandex-clad buttocks. Besides, looking for a way to ease my effort seemed counter to the reason I signed up to ride 224 miles. However, today was an entirely different proposition. I was now willing to stare at anything to ease the brutality of the elements.

When you meet other cyclists wearing skintight polyester jerseys with zippers down to the belly button, Velcro shoes, and shorts that leave nothing to the imagination, you tend to find a sort of camaraderie that requires no introduction. I found the first paceline I could and joined right in.

As I nestled in the funnel, the flock of riders shielded me from the viciousness of the wind. The warmth and comfort given by these twenty strangers was glorious. Drafting is a perfect metaphor for community. The gift of being carried by others contrasted with the frustration of submitting my will to the leader who was setting the pace. The strong take turns at the front, fighting the tempest for the village. When we move together, we're always affected by the consequences of each other's actions. Like every community, trust is required. If one falls, we all fall.

In life and on the bike, I find communities outgrow me, and I them. And so I spent that first day in absolute misery, vacillating between the frustration of submitting to the pain of going it alone and the boredom of the paceline. I just wanted to go home.

It was 4:00 p.m. when I spotted the Ohio River on the Kentucky state border and wheeled across that day's finish line at an old high school whose gymnasium would provide our night's lodging. My riding partner for the last two hours informed me that his heart rate monitor estimated he burned eight thousand calories that day. We certainly ate enough food to validate his calculations.

After six hours of rest and gorging, I staggered off to bed. Out of the shadows of a barren hallway, a new arrival's raspy voice greeted me. He was stocky and at most four-foot-ten. His skin was a leathered olive brown, illuminating his Eskimo ancestry. Beyond his thick glasses resided a deep soul with a friendly smile. He wore clothing more akin to that of a homeless man than a cyclist. Of the three thousand people who participated in the day's 112-mile torture, he was among the first to start out and the last to finish. My new friend had apparently been riding for almost seventeen hours. According to Jesus's upside-down kingdom language, my new friend was actually first. I was well versed in the cutting-edge method he employed, as this was the way my father and I used to climb the giant mountains of Colorado: painfully slowly. I should have known I was standing in the presence of greatness, yet I almost overlooked what this vanguard would have to teach me.

"Did the wind die down?" I inquired.

"Not really. But the stars came out. I hardly needed my lights."

"Were you really riding all day?"

"Yeah. It always takes me a while. I just take my time and enjoy the ride."

"There was nothing to enjoy today. That wind was awful!"

"Just made the ride more interesting."

"Interesting?" I snapped in disbelief.

"Oh, sure. It just creates a new set of challenges. If you think this was bad, you should have seen the weather a couple years ago. We had wind *and* rain. It took me even longer."

"And you came back?"

"Sure. It doesn't have to be bad. Did you see the new foliage in the mountain pass?"

"No, I didn't see anything. That was about the worst ride ever. I hated every minute of it."

He paused, lowered his glasses, and looked me over as if I'd just criticized his dog. "The wind's okay. You just have to accept that the ride is going to take a little longer." He slowed his words and spoke in a gentle whisper. "God's power is on display, you know. Just submit to it and enjoy yourself. Find the freedom."

"Enjoy it?" I started to smirk. "I'll find freedom when I get to go home."

He just smiled and asked where to lay his sleeping bag. I stumbled off to bed.

The next day was much of the same. The only changes were my sore legs, worn patience, and windburned cheeks. Eventually, the hours and miles passed with a blur of cyclists.

It must have been mile 60 when my paceline whizzed past the short-statured man I had met the night before and the clanging of his gadget-outfitted ride. Serious cyclists never attach a horn and cooler to their bikes. In fact, he was probably the only person out there who had a kickstand. I decided to leave the group and joined his five-mile-per-hour pace (my six-year-old son could have walked faster). He was smiling like a bewildered madman, clearly happy to see me. Apparently, he had only slept a couple of hours and left at 2:00 in the morning. Eager for company, he informed me of the turtles in the nearby stream bobbing their heads and the hawk above riding the wind.

"Watch the hawk, brother. The wind is his friend!" he shouted through the howling gusts.

"The wind's no friend of mine," I said with a laugh.

"What a glorious day to be riding. I was thinking about an old quote from John Muir, 'I only went out for a walk and finally concluded to stay out till sundown, for in going out, I found, was really going in.'[1] Looks like today I'll be going for more than sundown." His laughter was muted by the wind.

"What?" I asked.

He just smiled with a knowing that challenged my soul.

I looked to the hawk as he practiced his dance. Low on the horizon, aiming his head toward the sun, he powerfully thrust his feathered body upward. Soon his labors brought him to an invisible peak. Quickly adjusting his angle, he succumbed to the force of the wind, gently gliding left, then right, down and up again. This majestic creature was playing. The man was right; it was beautiful. The hawk's example of effort and grace would soon become my metaphor for the spiritual disciplines.

We rode together in silence until I could take no more of his pace. A sign for espresso gave me an out. "A cup of joe awaits me up ahead," I shouted as I waved good-bye.

"Good-bye friend, good-bye . . ." Our grand companion, the wind, quickly stole his voice.

Sometimes when I read the Bible I find myself tempted to imitate Thomas Jefferson and take scissors to the parts that don't suit me. One of the first passages to hit the blade would be Paul's words to slaves. In his letter to the people of Ephesus, he has the gall to suggest that slaves should serve their masters with respect and fear. I like to think that Jesus had started a revolution, that justice was to reign as he ushered in his kingdom on earth. Few evils in our world parallel the institution of slavery. I believe God would like to see slavery in all forms abolished. So I want Paul to denounce the social evil of slavery, not affirm it. I want hardcore restitution called out. I've been mining this verse for a couple of years now, and I wonder if Paul's call was really about setting the slaves free after all. I'm starting to think that maybe he was offering a key to internal freedom, the type of freedom that can never be stolen. Do our external circumstances always dictate the level of freedom we feel? Can we find freedom through submission?

A few miles down the road, something clicked. My slow, crazy friend's example began to make sense. It was clear that no matter how much I fought on this trip, I was not going to get my own way. Slowing my cadence, I pondered a new solution to my predicament.

What if I submitted to this pain? After all, submission is one of the disciplines.

What if I welcomed my invisible nemesis?

Could giving up be a spiritual practice?

Could I find freedom in my misery?

Within minutes of mustering a feeble attempt to embrace the wind, I noticed a shift.

Unconsciously, I had spent the entire trip tightly clenching my muscles in order to fight the wind, wasting priceless energy. For the next couple of miles I tried to loosen my body by methodically moving my neck and arms about. Something incredible happened. I suddenly became relaxed, and instead of perceiving the violently rushing air as my enemy, I began to imagine it as the presence of the Holy Spirit engulfing me.

I stopped staring at my speedometer and the gradually ticking miles. My pace slowed as I soaked in the dancing wheat fields and bending trees. For the remaining miles that day, I practiced the ancient discipline of submitting, and in her might, the wind sung the song of God's power and love, fierce yet freeing.

I'm sort of embarrassed to admit this, but it actually shocked me to see that my spiritual life could be practiced in the midst of that insanely awful trip. I didn't expect to find a way to actively practice a spiritual discipline in the windy, scorched Ohio farmland. For some reason I was under the illusion that spiritual activities and lessons had to come from books and speakers and that there were special ways that we practiced the disciplines, but they could not come from meeting a strange man riding his bike in rural Ohio, watching birds, and giving in to the wind.

That day on the bike, the anonymous sage showed me how to find freedom in the wind, but maybe more importantly, he showed me how to practice spiritual disciplines in the midst of life circumstances.

And by the time the man who drafted God finally finished his two-day trek, the staff of the bike tour had long since packed up and gone home. He finished with no fanfare, no roaring crowd, not even a volunteer to offer a drink when he pulled into downtown Columbus. Only his loyal friend, the wind, who had shepherded him the entire trip, was there rustling the trash in applause.

It seemed as if the discipline of submission had found me. Up until that point, all I had done for this project was begin thinking about practicing the disciplines, and all of a sudden the opportunity presented itself. Not to mention, it came as I was doing an activity I normally wouldn't have thought of as having any spiritual value. Could I break free from typical methods? Could I practice the disciplines in interesting and unusual ways? Maybe I could get creative with this project. The following week I decided to try.

When I told my family about the project, my daughter seemed really interested in what I was doing, which led me to a strange thought: What if I spent an entire day donating my complete attention to my nine-year-old daughter and four-year-old son by submitting entirely to their will? I am a fairly engaged dad, but parenting is an area of my life where I almost always feel like a failure, particularly in spiritual matters. This exercise seemed like not only the perfect opportunity to give a little spiritual teaching to my kids but also a solid chance to learn more about my chronic desire to have my own way.

After setting a budget and clarifying just how much candy and travel could be involved, I tried to explain to the kids the spiritual significance of submission, but they were so filled with Disney-like enthusiasm and excitement that I'm not really sure they heard anything I had to say. At least I tried, right?

In the following days they planned the schedule for our event, and my learning immediately began. I really struggled to avoid dropping manipulative suggestions as they decided to spend the day at an outdoor zoo during twenty-degree weather and a freak spring snowstorm. My unease continued as I heard rumor of potentially squeezing in a visit to Chuck E. Cheese's. This day would surely challenge my resolve.

As the snowy zoo, crowded pizza place day began, I was surprised to instantly feel an air of freedom in my submission. I didn't have to make decisions or be responsible for the outcomes. I didn't have to wrangle everyone to get out the door; if we were late, it didn't matter. The day wasn't about me. My only task was to give my undivided attention and to try to do so with a reasonably positive attitude. As a result, the usual anxiety that I tend to bring to family outings was pleasantly absent.

I've been noticing over the last few years that the things and circumstances I want often leave me unfulfilled and unhappy, while situations I don't want turn out to be not only good teachers but also sometimes even fun. In recent years I've been coming to the conclusion that I have very little idea what's going to be good for me. I think I know what I want, but historically, some of the best things for me I never would have chosen.

That day as we watched the freezing animals, I encountered a deep serenity from surrendering my desires and accepting life for what it is and not what I want it to be. I think this same peace comes when I accept people for who they are and not who I want them to be. Strangely, I found myself able to joyfully collapse my will into providence. When I let go, God shows up.

The frigid zoo wasn't too bad. As it turned out, we were the only people willing to visit the creatures on that cold day, so we had the place all to ourselves. And while Chuck E. Cheese's was filled to capacity and the sound decibel was at least that of a concert, I actually enjoyed the two-hour frenzy.

But on the drive home, I was left with the frightening realization that by surrendering my desire to have my own way, I was in fact giving my kids free rein to have their own way. What was good for my soul may have actually been bad parenting. I tried to salvage the situation by explaining to the kids all I had learned and the freedom we can experience by submitting to God. I think they were too sugared up to hear my teaching.

When the day was over, I began wondering about what happens when we're given the power to have our own way. One of the greatly ignored ironies of our day is the apparent consequences of attaining the cultural prize of wealth and fame. Few things stack the statistical cards in our favor for divorce, drug addiction, depression, and suicide like having wealth or notoriety. The misery of the rich and famous is well documented. With all the freedom money can buy, people so often live in bondage to themselves, their image, and the world we have created for them. In contrast, according to the biblical account of Matthew, Jesus gave a strange farming analogy about being yoked to him. (A yoke is a plowing device that binds two oxen together so that the stronger one can lead and train the weaker.) Essentially, Jesus was saying, "Chain yourself to me, and I'll teach you how to live as you were created to live." He said, "My yoke is easy and my burden is light."[2] Jesus knew that as humans, we are by nature slaves—slaves to power, slaves to approval, slaves to escapism. So instead of leaving us bound to our selfish desires, he calls us to chain ourselves to his rule of love. Freedom through submission. In a sense, that sums up the spiritual disciplines. On this day I learned that voluntarily letting go was one way to be free from my oppressive desire to have my own way.

Later that night my daughter reflected, "Dad, I think it's really cool that you submitted to someone else for the day. I think I want to try that. What if I gave my whole day to my brother and just played with him all day long?"

Funny, for all the talking I did, it was my example that she ended up hearing.

Submission
Saint Patrick (390–460)

Patrick, patron saint of Ireland, was actually British. At age sixteen, Patrick was kidnapped and forced into slavery in Ireland. After six years of slavery, through a precarious and providential series of events, Patrick escaped and returned home to England.

Once home, Patrick began having visions in which Irish voices called out to him, "We beg you to come and walk among us once more." Clearly Patrick had no interest in returning to a land where he had been a slave, but the visions persisted, with Christ speaking to him in the vision, saying, "He who gave his life for you, he it is who speaks within you." Eventually Patrick submitted to the dangerous call of returning to Ireland.

Stories of Patrick and his work among the people of Ireland abound. And while what is fact and what is myth is unclear, what is known is that his missional work altered the culture so drastically that he's still celebrated some 1,500 years later. Some scholars even believe that had Patrick not introduced the teachings of Jesus to Ireland, the monasteries would not have been founded, and therefore much of the classical literature of the Greeks and Romans would have been lost during Europe's dark ages.

Even today, the historic Celtic Christian communities have much to offer Western Christianity.

Understanding

Fasting

Fasting is the voluntary denial of an otherwise normal function for the sake of intense spiritual activity. Remember, there is nothing wrong with these normal functions in life; it is just that there are times when we set them aside in order to concentrate. Once we understand this, we can see both the reasonableness of fasting as well as the broader dimensions to it.

Ordinarily we think of fasting from food, which is the normal way the Bible speaks of it. But we can fast from many things. We can fast from media. We can fast from noise, hurry, and crowds. We can fast from excessive talk. We can fast from our technological devices, our computers and our cell phones and more. Whatever in our lives is producing an addiction in us is a prime area for fasting. In this way we are learning to depend upon God alone.

Throughout Scripture, fasting is a well-recognized spiritual discipline ranging from Daniel's partial fast[1] to Jesus's absolute fast.[2] The list of biblical personages who fasted reads like a "who's who" of Scripture: Abraham's servant when he was seeking a bride for Isaac; Moses on Mount Sinai; Hannah when she prayed for a child; David on two separate occasions; Elijah after his victory over Jezebel; Ezra when he was mourning Israel's faithlessness; Nehemiah as he was preparing for the trip back to Israel; Esther when God's people were threatened with extermination; Daniel on numerous occasions; the people of Nineveh, including the cattle (involuntarily, no doubt); Jesus as he began his public ministry; Paul at the point of his conversion; the Christians at Antioch as they sent off Paul and Barnabas for their mission endeavor; Paul and the others as they appointed elders in all the churches; and more. In his teaching on the subject, Jesus simply assumed that the children of the kingdom would fast and was giving instruction on how it could be done with spiritual success.[3]

Not only that, but many of the great Christians throughout history fasted: Martin Luther and John Calvin, John Knox and John Wesley, Jonathan Edwards and Charles Finney, and many, many others.

We fast for many reasons. We fast because it reveals the things that control us. We fast because it helps to give us balance in life. We fast because there is an urgent need. Most important of all, we fast because God calls us to it. We have heard the *kol Yahweh*, the voice of the Lord, and we must obey.

In Jesus's day, fasting was a well-understood practice. Today, however, there is an abysmal ignorance of even the most elementary aspects of fasting. Hence, we need basic instruction in how to go about fasting: how we begin a fast, how long we should fast, how much water we need to drink during a fast, how we break a fast, and much more.

While the physical aspects of fasting intrigue us, we need to remember that the major work of fasting is in the realm of the spirit. The spiritual discipline of fasting can bring breakthroughs in the heart and mind that will not happen in any other way. It is a means of God's grace for the continuing formation of the human personality into the likeness of Christ.

Richard J. Foster

Fasting

Hunger in Dark Rooms

> What could there be about a shadow that was so terrible
> . . . that would chill her with a fear that was beyond
> shuddering, beyond crying or screaming, beyond the
> possibility of comfort?
>
> Madeleine L'Engle[1]

My world is built on pursuing and satisfying my every need and desire—after all, I am an American. When I have a headache, I take medicine. When I'm tired, I go to bed. When I'm hot, I turn on the air conditioner, and when I'm hungry, I eat. The notion of voluntarily depriving myself of anything that is readily accessible feels ridiculous. Not only do I get nervous about the suffering associated with fasting, but I'm increasingly uncomfortable with the mix of motives it brings up.

A friend recently told me that she thought a spiritual food fast was nearly impossible to do in this day and age because of our obsession with dieting. Certainly America's obsession with outward appearance borderlines on psychotic. Not only do we spend enough money each year on diets to end global starvation, but we're just getting more obese. According to my readings, in a five-day fast I could lose a good ten pounds. While I'm not really overweight, slimming down a little sounded great. Approaching fasting, or any discipline for that matter, with nothing but spiritual motives was potentially going to be extremely problematic for me. I'm a mess of motives in most everything I do. I'm not sure I'm capable of doing *anything* with pure intention. There was a time when I felt such judgment about my selfish motives that I couldn't bring myself to admit they even existed. Doesn't hiding from things make them go away? Of course, like most lies, this denial stood in direct contrast to the truth. I've since come to believe that concealing issues only makes the beast stronger.

Confession is a small death of self. I offered mine to my dad.

"You've got to help me out with this, Dad. How am I supposed to fast with pure motives? I don't do anything with pure intent."

My admission ignited his laughter. He bellowed like he always does, deep and contagious. I waited patiently for a good thirty seconds while he entertained himself with my penance. I already felt relieved.

"Nate, that's all of us. No one approaches the disciplines with anything but jumbled motives. So let me tell you how I handled this problem." He sat up straight, raised his chin, and pursed his lips, displaying his piety. "I once decided to quit praying out loud until I got my motives straight. No one would hear me pray until I could do so with pure intention. The result was that I quit praying altogether. The experience totally immobilized my ability to pray."

"Are you serious? Nice." It was my turn to offer a small absolution in the form of laughter. "But come on, Dad! You've got to help me here. You're the discipline guru."

"Yeah, right!" Dad grinned. "Wait a minute. Maybe I do have something for you."

Sifting through some papers on his desk, Dad pulled out a sheet and began to read a passage he had just written:

> The human heart itself is part of our problem. We are, each and every one of us, a tangled mass of motives: hope and fear, faith and doubt, simplicity and duplicity, honesty and falsity, openness and guile. God knows our heart in ways we can never know. Supernatural abilities are needed to untangle the mess. God is the only one who can separate the true from the false. Only God can purify the motives of the heart.[2]

After a moment I responded, "This is helpful, because I can't seem to escape the idea that I'd like to knock off a few pounds. I keep reading about how detoxing the body can be a really positive thing too. Besides, regular fasting would sure make me cool with my yoga friends."

Dad smiled. "Periodically fasting is great for cleaning out your body, although I wouldn't think of it as a weight loss plan. You gain back the weight when you start eating again. Think of fasting as a way to gain control over an aspect of our lives that our culture seems to have no self-control over—food. Christian fasting keeps God in mind. You don't wait to get your intention pure. The experience itself is a way to clear motives, as are the other disciplines. Just approach it with honesty and pray that God will purify your heart."

That helped with my motives, but there was still the issue of suffering.

Cradling my coffee, I lamented my dread to a friend.

"Oh, I love fasting!" she hastily responded with bulging eyes and fire-hose enthusiasm. "Nothing turns the volume up on God's voice like fasting. Everything becomes so clear."

For the next ten minutes I sat mesmerized by her fervor. My curiosity was stirred, and I started a five-day fast the following week.

Day One

As soon as I began, I found a particular character liability useful: stubbornness. Once I commit to a task and fully remove the option of quitting, my body concedes. I've seen this happen when I've climbed fourteen-thousand-foot mountains and when I've ridden hundreds of miles on my bike. It's as if I fight the skirmish days before the event with the slow accumulation of mental resolve. I was convinced the only requirement for completing a five-day fast would be iron-clad determination; I was totally unprepared for what this experience would uncover.

Things started relatively easy—uncomfortable, but certainly doable. For some reason I had long held the belief that if I missed a meal, my blood sugar would drop and I might detonate, or at least be incapacitated in bed. Neither happened. In fact, I was able to go about my day in pretty normal fashion. A couple of times I momentarily forgot that I was fasting and started to shove a chip into my mouth. How unsettling to think that I might go about the day unconsciously consuming food left in my sight. Isn't eating a conscious choice? Was cramming food in my mouth whenever possible a habit I had spent years cultivating?

In spite of how well the fast was going, I found it nearly impossible to motivate myself to do any spiritual activities. That night I decided to make this not a spiritual fast but rather a first step in learning about the process. I could always save the 4:00 a.m. prayer vigil for another fast. For now, living with mild suffering and resisting the temptation to be cranky was labor enough.

Day Two

I awoke refreshed and excited, like I had a new toy to play with. I found confidence brewing in the knowledge that I could actually live without constantly eating.

To my surprise, I was still able to ride my bike, though of course at a much slower pace.

I had a subtle headache much of the day, and my stomach roared with angst. "Easy, friend, easy!" I whispered to the restless horse in my belly.

I once heard my brother's priest say that fasting is good for the soul but bad for the family. I determined not to keep up the fast if I was going to be destructive to others. Apparently, one of the benefits of fasting is that it helps you become aware of problem areas in your life. Creating a mess with my family isn't worth it to me, and honestly I don't need help knowing what I suck at. While it was requiring considerable effort to go about life as normal, I was doing okay. My kids were impressed. Evidently my daughter had also thought missing a meal would cause a person to spontaneously combust.

Normally, I'm able to have an hour or two to myself late at night. This evening my discretionary time brought on relentless boredom. Restless and unmotivated, I found it impossible to focus. I tried to sit in it. I tried to remember the gift of stillness. Instead I proceeded to spend a couple of hours online, bought a bunch of stuff I didn't need, made sexual advances toward my wife, and went to bed.

I spent an agitated night frightened by images of Gandhi unable to stand without help. That new-toy feeling was shifting to dread.

Day Three

Despite my evening angst, I arose the next morning unassisted and feeling decent. Throughout the day, my headache and hunger were gradually replaced with a mild euphoria and a profound stillness. A soft spiritual awareness covered me. You know how in movies they slow down a fight scene so the enlightened hero is able to deliver blows with precision and grace? It was like that, without the violence. My friend was right: the volume on God was turned up.

I abandoned myself and submitted to the process. Lost in wordless prayer, I spent much of the day perspiring with love for God and others.

I seemed to have stumbled upon a sort of rhythm to the fast. That night the pain and boredom subsided, my thoughts were sharp and clear, and I felt super mellow.

All of this came in spite of my failure to try to make this a spiritual activity. Why am I surprised God would nudge his way in, undeterred by my deliberate choice not to pursue him? I guess that's the way of love.

Day Four

The previous day's spiritually laced rhythm continued. My steps were light, almost as if I didn't exist. I felt powerful, like I could accomplish anything. I occasionally thought of food, yet I felt I could fast indefinitely. I half wanted to. I was dizzy when I stood up and my tongue felt funny, but I was on an adventure, curious as to what lay ahead.

I had lost five pounds. I tried not to care, but I did. I tried to not look in the mirror, but I did. I began thinking about how I used food. I ate because I thought I had to in order to avoid passing out or being irritable with everyone. Truth is, I often ate for pleasure and because food was there and I was expected to consume it. I used food to escape, reward myself, fill the spaces in my life, and relieve social anxiety. Eating for life-giving sustenance wasn't a thought I had ever considered. This experience was changing my relationship with food.

As evening approached, my spiritual levity subsided and darkness rolled in. I was done with work, and Christy was out with the kids. I had the evening free and alone, an extremely rare occasion. It started with a restlessness. I couldn't seem to make a decision on how to spend my time. I tried to read and couldn't concentrate. TV didn't hold my attention, the internet was down, and music was uninteresting. I called a few friends; no one answered. I cleaned the toilets, scrubbed the sinks, took out the trash, and collapsed on the bed stricken with anxiety.

Then an unnamed, surreal fear came rolling over me in waves and crashing ashore on the beach of my consciousness. I had nothing. I was alone. Drowning in emptiness, I felt tears bubble up. I began swimming through a series of painful memories, revealing the scabs of emotional wounds. The undertow ripped away my thin protective cover; I was naked with grief. The saltwater penetrated, stinging and festering; emotional pus oozed about.

The memories tumbled down: me at four years old, immobilized with sadness. I sat in the middle of a room while the other kids laughed and played. I didn't want to exist. During grade school recesses I sat perched upon a wooden structure on the edge of a playground, methodically polishing a rough rock. The dying leaves of fall danced about. Day after day I imagined life was a theatrical drama, and my part was ending.

Deeper, darker I swam, paging through the scrapbook of torn and fuzzy pictures I've spent my life collecting. Desperately I tried to make sense of vague memories of abuse and the accompanying emotions: fear, dread, terror, guilt, shame, shattered innocence, and the birth of self-hatred. Clouded in mystery, the memories and emotions cascaded down. I felt the horror of recurring childhood nightmares, of waking up covered in sweat, left alone, rocking myself back to sleep with no one to care for me.

And then I felt the pain of my part: anger, rage, cruelty toward others, brooding resentments, self-harm, and the haze of years spent drinking and drugging. Frantically I'd tried to buy time. Anything to outrun what sometimes felt like my inescapable destiny of eventually ending my own life.

I cried myself to sleep, determined to end the fast in the morning.

Roxy's is a small breakfast diner. The entrance is through the kitchen, where you're greeted by the morning's stack of dirty dishes and a heavily tattooed cook. The menu is attached to the table, and the walls are covered with colorful slogans reminding you that your ability to eat there is contingent upon your positive attitude. This is where I broke my fast, though later I wished I'd heeded my dad's advice about returning to eating with a light meal to avoid unwanted trips to the bathroom.

I had no idea what had happened to me the previous night. I'm prone to be a bit dramatic, but that was just weird. I didn't know I still had all that in me or that not eating could bring about such an emotional reaction. Yet there it was: fasting had in fact revealed something hidden, something for me to work through.

I suspected my experience was both unusual and potentially another step in my healing. But I wasn't ready to face what the fasting had brought up; it would have to wait.

It was time to try an easier discipline.

A Portrait of

Fasting
Sundar Singh (1889–1929)

Sundar was born in northern India to a Sikh family. When he was fourteen, his mother died, launching him into violence and despair. Much of his anger was directed at Christians, and he went so far as to publicly burn a Bible. A few years later, Sundar decided to kill himself. The evening of his planned suicide, he had a vision of Jesus. He immediately converted to Christianity and was denounced by his family. Later in his life, however, people began to call him Sadhu, a Hindu name for a wandering holy man. It was important to Sundar to present Jesus within the Indian cultural context. Upon facing opposition from the Western church, he stated, "Indians do need the Water of Life, but not in the European cup."[3]

Fasting was an important part of Sundar's life. He felt that the weaker his body grew when he fasted, the more spiritually attentive he became. To emulate Jesus, he went out into the forest and fasted for forty days. During this fast, he saw Christ in a "spiritual vision, with pierced hands, bleeding feet, and a radiant face."[4] During Sundar's times of praying in the forest, he apparently had an ongoing conversation with Jesus. He recorded the exchange in his tender book *At the Master's Feet*.

Sundar's missional work took him to Malaysia, Japan, China, Israel, Europe, and Australia, earning him the title "the apostle with the bleeding feet and burning heart." Sundar journeyed many times through the Himalayan Mountains to Tibet. On one such trek through in 1929, he disappeared and was never heard from again.

Understanding
Study

Study is the process whereby our minds take on an order conforming to the order of whatever we concentrate upon. Garbage in, garbage out; or conversely, beauty in, beauty out. It really is as simple as that. This is why the wise old apostle Paul urged us to set our minds on "whatever is true, whatever is honorable, whatever is just, whatever is pure, whatever is pleasing, whatever is commendable."[1]

What makes study a Christian spiritual discipline is the *content* of our study as well as the *spirit* by which we engage in our study.

The content of our study consists in all those things that lead to the glory of God. For the Christian, our study focuses primarily upon two great "books": Scripture and "the book of nature." With regard to Scripture, we begin by quieting ourselves until we can be attentive to the Word in Scripture. Then: We read. We reflect. We absorb. We allow Scripture to read us. We apply Scripture to our living. With regard to nature, the process is much the same, except that our "reading" comes by way of observing and listening. Then: We reflect. We absorb. We allow nature to read us. We apply the lessons of nature to our living.

The spirit in which we engage in our study is an overall spirit of humility. We come with open hands and open heart. We become subject to the subject matter. We come as student, not teacher. We come as wholehearted learners. We stand *under* the text of Scripture, *under* the book of nature. Without this pervasive spirit of humility, study will only produce arrogance in us. A haughty spirit undermines humility of heart. Arrogance and a teachable spirit are mutually exclusive.

There are four well-recognized steps in study. The first is *repetition*. Repetition regularly channels our minds in a specific direction, thus ingraining habits of thought. Ingrained habits of thought can be formed by repetition alone, thus changing behavior, even if we do not understand what is being repeated.

The second step in study is *concentration*. Concentration centers our minds. It clears away the clutter of a thousand stimuli and forces us to focus on one thing only. This focus allows us to be truly present where we are.

Comprehension is the third step in the discipline of study. All of us have had the experience of reading something over and over and then, all of a sudden, we understand what it means. This "eureka" experience of understanding catapults us to a new level of growth and freedom. It brings insight and discernment.

The final step in study is *reflection*. While comprehension defines what we are studying, reflection defines the *significance* of what we are studying. Reflection allows us to see things from God's perspective.

Study produces joy. Like any novice, we will find it hard work in the beginning. But as our proficiency grows, so will our joy. Study is a discipline ordained by God for the training of the mind in "righteousness and peace and joy in the Holy Spirit."[2]

Richard J. Foster

Study

Practicing My Failures

> We need to understand that Jesus is a *thinker*, that
> this is not a dirty word but an essential work, and that
> his other attributes do not preclude thought, but only
> ensure that he is certainly the greatest thinker of the
> human race: "the most intelligent person who ever lived
> on earth."
>
> Dallas Willard[1]

I occasionally have lunch with a colleague who teaches drama.
Over plastic trays smattered with small-town college cafeteria
cuisine and the noise of a crowded dining commons, we've had
many interesting, inspiring, and intense talks. Paul Patton cares
too much about me and the subjects we discuss to follow traditional conversational etiquette. With passion usually reserved
for the stage, he'll move in close and loudly enunciate. His face
tenses and relaxes in a rhythmic ebb and flow while his body
reverberates verbal nuances like a well-crafted blues line. With
this sort of intensity, he gifts me with lengthy recitations from
poets, Old Testament prophets, and media theorists.

One day I asked him about his incredible ability to recite long passages. Apparently memorization didn't come naturally to him; it is the fruit of a longtime daily discipline. Each morning Paul works through his current passage and reviews a few he memorized previously. Paul spoke of this ritual as the most important part of his day, as it often birthed lengthy journal entries and spontaneous prayer. Paul's thirty-year reservoir of digested words provided a life-sustaining buoy during a recent depressive storm. "It was so dark, Nate," he told me. "Day after day all I had was words I'd long ago ingested."

Whether Paul realized it or not, it seems memorizing various texts, biblical and otherwise, had been his means of spiritual formation. As his recent crisis showed, he was able to respond when he needed to respond. He had developed reliable tools that nurtured him when he needed them to.

Paul's instructions to me were simple: "Let a passage find you. When a quote or line resonates in your soul, scribble it down, and if it keeps coming back to you, then you should clock the hours and consume it. Memorization is like working a muscle—the more you exercise it, the easier it becomes."

Of course, the discipline of study can be practiced in a number of ways. At certain seasons in my life, I've no longer found it beneficial to keep reading or listening to lectures. Gathering information is not what I lack; it's the practice and application that I need. Taking time to soak in what I've already heard feels like an important part of the learning process. I once heard my dad remark that he wondered if people just go from reading one book to the next but never really living with the work. I can be greedy with learning, collecting and storing knowledge like a compulsive hoarder. And for what? To impress others? To feel clever and smug? Tightly wrapped in a cloak of quotes and insights, like an addict I detach from others and life in order to consume more. And to what end?

I needed study to be something simple and practical. Paul's enthusiasm piqued my interest in memorization. A way to practice this discipline had found me. Within a week I had my piece and was ready to begin.

Each morning I set a timer for fifteen minutes to read, recite, and write my lines over and over again. I carried a note card with my lines written on it. When I felt the card in my pocket, I would turn my attention, however briefly, to the words. I went so far as to rubber band the card to my bike handlebars so that on my commute to work I could whisper the lines. I focused my attention. I pondered the meaning and significance. I clocked the hours.

According to Joshua Choonmin Kang's excellent book *Scripture by Heart*, fifteen minutes a day would make memorizing one chapter per week manageable for most people.[2] After two weeks of work, this is what I could recite from memory:

So here's what I want you to do, God helping you: Take your everyday, ordinary life—your sleeping, eating, going-to-work, and walking-around life—and place it before God as an offering. Embracing what God does for you is the best thing you can do for him.[3]

I was frustrated. Shouldn't I have been able to memorize a whole lot more than a couple of skimpy lines? I knew my memory wasn't one of my strong features, but this was ridiculous. All that time to collect only a handful of words! Granted, after four years with the same phone number, I still couldn't remember it, not to mention that I have to write everything down or it seems to escape me completely. My to-do list includes things as mundane as to shave and eat, otherwise I'll forget. Yet for some reason I thought things would be different if I really applied myself.

I just couldn't seem to escape the obsession with being productive. I'm always trying to get more done quicker, and when I can't clearly see my progress, I get irritated. Feeding my driven angst is my compliance to the sin of comparison and its subtle, destructive fruit, competition. Isn't rivalry the root of the first biblical murder? Yet for us it's a cultural virtue and the fuel that drives our economy. I often find it lurking in the corners of my consciousness, motivating so much of what I do. Born out of comparison is this drive to be perfect, or at a minimum really good, at the things I do. Being in the learning process is embarrassing. I want to hide, or at least pretend I'm really better than I am.

The disciplines can potentially free me from my need to be perfect, can't they? I try. I learn. Ultimately I get to grow. Yet, I'm learning, this silly need to achieve can take a long time to surgically remove. Through the years I continue working with this lesson. Occasionally I stumble across the beauty of letting go of my need to be good at things. I am loved. I have nothing to prove. God's love and acceptance frees me from our culture's obsessive need to succeed or impress. Not to mention that being good at something or marking progress isn't the point of the spiritual disciplines, right? Besides, I'm pretty inept at measuring my progress anyway. My dad had taught me, "Slow and steady wins the race." Even though study wasn't a race, he was right. Anything I had become good at happened not overnight but slowly, steadily, by repetition. It seemed to take me years to integrate lessons. Again, isn't it that competitive drive that tells me that because I've been confronted with this lesson before, I should have learned it already? Yet grace understands my humanness. Grace gives me space to keep going, appreciate the process, and accept what I lack.

I decided to address my desire to only do things that I'm good at by facing something I had wanted so badly to learn but felt I had failed at so many times that I had all but concluded it was an impossible mission. I wanted to learn grammar and how to write a complete sentence. Could I possibly make this process a spiritual discipline?

Is it okay for an author and a professor to confess he can't recognize a complete sentence? I was one of those students with a learning disability who was sharp enough to fake my way through traditional education without notice. Please don't assume because of this that I have worked for shoddy institutions or been coddled through school and publishing. I've learned to hide, to fool and pretend, and ultimately to overcompensate, kind of like how a fire juggler could be so amazing that you wouldn't even notice his singed hair. Smoke and mirrors. My kind wife proofreads everything I write; few people have ever read a long email from me without her first cleaning it up. It's been hard not to be jealous of people who can write a book in a year or a slew of emails in an hour. I've learned to be concise. I'm notorious for my one-sentence email responses that I'm sure still take me longer to write than it takes others to write half a page.

When I was first hired as a professor nine years ago, I went to a learning center for help. I paid the money and took the test. I then proceeded to convince myself I didn't have the time to follow through. The truth was, I was so embarrassed that I never returned.

It was time to face my inadequacy.

The ceiling was high and the wood floors creaked in the old university building. The air was filled with mystery and the smell of musty, worn books. I sat in the waiting room with palms perspiring, stomach in knots, rocking my feet back and forth like a child waiting for the principal. Dr. Kimberly Moore-Jumonville was the chair of my university's English department and the tutor to whom I had chosen to reveal my secret incompetence.

Her smile and enthusiasm were slightly disarming as I was welcomed into her office and offered a reupholstered Victorian sitting chair fit for teatime with a wealthy British woman. Front and center, perched on an ornate copper stand, was a hundred-pound dictionary opened to the Qs. Clearly it wasn't just for decoration. My anticipation heightened every time the old heating boiler pinged like the cogs of a roller coaster climbing to a five-hundred-foot drop. I took a deep breath, readjusted my clothes, gripped the edge of my seat, and sunk into the droning tones of Mozart softly echoing from the corner. She handed me a small grammar book; on the back it stated, "For ages 7–10."

The ride began.

For the next year we met weekly. I started with verbs, then tackled adjectives and adverbs. I had worksheets and reading assignments to complete every week. Repetition. Slowly and steadily I faced one of my childhood failures.

Kimberly was a wonderful teacher—so patient, so encouraging, always supportive, and always filled with grace. Quickly my dread shifted to enthusiasm. Within a few months my embarrassment was replaced with tears of gratitude. What I had honestly thought to be impossible was happening: I was learning grammar.

Kimberly created the perfect space to invite me into the discipline of study. Teaching with grace and care was the discipline she had spent the last twenty years crafting. Her practice of educational hospitality had become so habitual that I doubt she was even aware she was doing it.

When I entered tutoring for English, I assumed I would be brought back into the rigid world of "correct and proper" ways of writing. I was more than surprised to learn how the rules were really an aid and could be broken and manipulated once understood. The doctor and I would launch into detailed conversations about words and language and how they enable us to convey the richness, beauty, and sorrow of the human experience.

Making this process a spiritual discipline happened naturally as my work kept bumping into God. My learning became a prayerful experience of wonder and amazement. "God, what does this mean? How can I use this? Teach me about the gift of language and how together we can creatively use it for good and beauty."

I was coming to see that the spiritual discipline of study could be applied to all sorts of areas. It was so easy to bring God into learning. I felt his delight in showing me how things work. His love for creativity was immensely evident.

Maybe the biggest takeaway I have from the experience is that it is possible for me to learn. If I'm not in a hurry or bound to having to be good at something, I feel I can learn just about anything.

♦ ♣ ♠

I'm part of a small group of guys who for the last five years have met weekly to listen and offer each other support. During a meeting a few weeks after my failure with memorizing, I was asked to share some ways in which I had been encountering God. I found myself talking about how I was becoming aware of God in activities in which I normally never would have thought of him. Rather than complaining about feeding the dog or washing dishes, I had been trying to offer my tasks as a time of worship, and I found myself awakening to God's presence in the ordinary. In spite of my perceived failure with memorizing, it was clear that the few lines I had spent two weeks on had snuck their way into my life.

This made me realize that learning to live a few lines is probably better then just memorizing a hundred. A friend once said, "If memorizing takes you a long time and feels like you're chiseling words in granite, rest easy, for words in granite will last."

My time with the discipline of study was a blend of frustration and wonder. I was so encouraged that I decided to revisit another seemingly impossible challenge, something I had failed at as a kid, something I wanted to be able to do but knew I didn't have any natural abilities for: I decided to learn to play bass guitar. Doesn't every teenage boy dream of being in a rock band? Midlife angst strikes again. Little did I know where it would take me.

Study

George Washington Carver (1864–1943)

Born into slavery in Diamond Grove, Missouri, George Washington Carver showed a strong interest in plants from early on. Even after slavery was abolished, he was not allowed to attend school until the age of fourteen. After graduating high school, Carver was denied admission to Highland College (KS) because of his race, but he was later accepted at Simpson College in Iowa, where he studied art. He went on to study agriculture at Iowa State, becoming the school's first African American graduate while earning both bachelor's and master's degrees.

Carver spent his entire career working and teaching at the Tuskegee Institute in Alabama, insisting that faith and science went hand in hand. He even referred to his lab as "God's little workshop."

Carver's agricultural knowledge was so highly thought of that he was offered higher paying jobs by the likes of Henry Ford and Thomas Edison, but he refused them, instead choosing to use his knowledge of agriculture to teach and educate poor, African American farmers in the South.

Carver famously addressed Congress in 1921, extolling the virtues of peanuts. When asked by one congressman how he learned what he knew, Carver replied, "From an old book . . . the Bible." The congressman asked, "Does the Bible tell about peanuts?" Carver replied, "No, Sir, but it tells about the God who made the peanut. I asked Him to show me what to do with the peanut, and He did."[14] Carver used the discipline of study to develop over one hundred products made from peanuts, including cosmetics, dyes, paints, plastics, gasoline, and nitroglycerin.

Interlude

Discipline Hazard #1:
The Self-Hatred Narrative

> An obsession merely with doing all God commands
> may be the very thing that rules out being the kind of
> person He calls us to be.
>
> Dallas Willard[1]

Her face revealed it all. She was wound like a carelessly cranked guitar string. Her intensity was both intimidating and exhilarating. I braced myself.

"Nate, I heard that you always quit doing spiritual activities for Lent. I think that is so fantastic! I mean, it's okay to take a break once in a while, right?"

I had no idea what she was talking about, and I wasn't entirely sure I even knew who she was. I smiled and nodded my head in agreement, and like a good professor pretended to be the expert. "Yeah, it's good to take a break. If the spiritual life doesn't lead us to freedom and grace, then we've probably missed the point."

Her face softened. She liked my response. I'm not sure I did.

It took me a while to figure out what she was talking about. Eventually I concluded she was referencing a comment I made at a dinner party when asked to pray. I didn't feel like praying, so I quickly smarted off, "Sorry, I quit praying for Lent." Everyone laughed and someone else prayed. It was meant as a joke and a little passive stab at my friends who diet for Lent.

I knew the anxiety she carried. Her eyes had a starving sort of look, a look Christians often wear. It's the face of someone who spends a lifetime striving to be the person they think they should be, chasing the approval of God and others, but never really feeling like they measure up. It's seen on the person who follows the rules, does everything leaders ask them to do, is seldom acknowledged for all their efforts, and feels guilty when they slack on a diligent devotional life. In the deep recesses of their heart, they can't seem to outrun the gnawing ache that they aren't good enough. When honest, they'll admit the lie that drives so much of their life: God is disappointed with their performance, just like everyone else is, just like their parents, teachers, spouse, and bosses were and are.

I'm truly impressed that these sorts of people stay in the faith, remaining committed year after year, showing up with the smile they think others expect of them. These people have a fortitude I lack. How they continue to teach Sunday school, host Bible studies, and organize potlucks and community outreach projects without tasting the unconditional love of God is baffling. They have my deep respect—and pity.

"Hey Dad, do you ever notice when you talk about the disciplines that most people just see them as another burden, something painful that they won't be able to accomplish, something failure-ridden and guilt inducing?"

"Oh, I hate that," he replied. "I get this often and I don't understand. They're missing the point entirely. The disciplines give more than they require. It's not about a list of things to do. It's about a life with God."

"But it is about things we do. We train, we do various exercises, right?"

"Yes, but we do them in a way that fits where we are in life. Do you know this quote by Abbot John Chapman? 'Pray as you can, not as you can't.' We're not trying to accomplish something; it's a cooperative relationship with God. We don't conquer the disciplines; they conquer us. They are grace that God uses to transform the human personality. God doesn't look to put heavy burdens on people or set them up to fail."

"So what do you say to people caught up in the doing, failure, guilt mentality?" I asked.

"Stop. Go for a walk. Watch a football game. Go about your day and in small, simple ways invite God into the everyday happenings of your life. Actually, this is where a spiritual friendship or director can be really helpful—someone who can guide you into a space where the disciplines are helpful, life-giving exercises." Dad paused, squinting his eyes as he peered into the distance. "You know, the classic writers wrote about the disciplines in two categories, via negative and via positive. Dallas [Willard] interpreted them as disciplines of engagement, meaning activities that you *begin* to do. He also spoke of disciplines of abstinence, meaning things you unplug from. People who feel overburdened should start with disciplines of abstinence and see where the journey takes them. Their discipline is only to quit trying and learn to be still before God, learn to bring him into the chaos of their lives. So many people just need to get through their day, and the last thing they need is more things they have to do. God invites them into a life, not a spiritual to-do list."

"Okay, that works. You know what part of the problem is for me? It's the word *discipline*. Who looks at that word as being positive? It conjures up such negative thoughts. I mean, isn't that the word we use when we talk about military boot camp or punishing a child? Isn't it the intimidating, authoritarian voice fixing to unleash some hurt? 'Teach these kids some discipline!' I know you've been trying to redeem the word," I said almost apologetically, "but I half wonder if for many people it's so ingrained as a negative that redemption is nearly impossible."

"It's a good word. It's not defined as negative in the classic sense. Some people use the term spiritual training or spiritual exercises."

"What about something like practices of grace?" I suggested. "Or habits of grace? Maybe intentional exercises of grace? Yeah, I like that one—intentional exercises of grace. What do you think, Dad?"

"Yeah, that works. But I like *discipline*. It's a good word."

"You're always going for classic definitions of words, aren't you?"

"I guess," he said with uneasy confidence and a soft grin.

In working with people for a number of years, I've heard a lot of stories . . . and secrets. I'm coming to believe that behind the fronts and facades, most people live with a sense of self-disdain. The details of the stories are different—for some it's what they've done or not done, for others it's who they have or haven't become—but the self-hatred narrative is almost always there. I don't think most people really like what they see in those honest, vulnerable moments when they look at themselves in the mirror.

It makes sense. We live in a culture that defines our value by what we accomplish, what we own, and how we look. I'm struck with the awareness that for the first time in the history of human existence, the majority of our social contact comes in the form of someone trying to sell us something. Is it just a coincidence that the basic message of the most dominant voice in our society is that we are in some way lacking? Mix in some good rugged individualism and constant pressure to do more, then try navigating life and the ever-increasing demand on our time and energy—these are the ingredients of our modern culture that has produced a collection of people deeply broken in ways our great-grandparents never could have imagined.

Self-disdain drives the myriad of addictions that affect almost everyone. Whether it's drugs, food, porn, video games, or our phones, we are obsessed with finding new ways to disconnect from life. So many of us spend our lives rehearsing the self-hatred narrative, desperately longing to escape who we are.

Oh, to be significant.

To be loved.

I bear similar wounds. I know all about the self-hatred narrative. When I first read Jesus's tale of the prodigal son, I just assumed the father's grace and acceptance were a one-shot deal. Because his father was so reckless in his forgiveness, I just assumed that the kid would live the rest of his life trying to prove he was now responsible and worthy of his dad's crazy decision to lavish him with love despite his rebellion. Of course, if he ever chose to return to his life of excess, he would never be welcomed home again. Or would he?

It wasn't that I didn't believe in God's love and grace, but I bought the lie that you only got to come home once, maybe twice if you were really sorry. And it went without saying that forgiveness of sins meant I had to immediately begin doing spiritual and moral activities. God's gift of grace had to be repaid with my works. I'm not saying that we shouldn't do spiritual activities and direct our movements to be pleasing toward God, but I was operating out of the subconscious assumption that God's continued love was contingent upon my behavior, as if I could make him stop loving me.

When I became a Christian, I quickly gravitated toward a church filled with people who never moved past viewing themselves as sinful creatures whose actions killed Jesus. The awfulness of humanity seemed to invade all the messages and songs; it fit well with the self-hatred narrative I'd been cultivating for years. I became an astute student of their culture of works and legalism. And so, out of a blend of obligation, guilt, and social pressure, I began working on the spiritual disciplines.

My exercises were fairly limited in their breadth. I did the usual evangelical activities: daily quiet time, reading and memorizing the Bible, tithing, attending two services a week, and submitting to church leaders. I was even able to successfully practice God's favorite discipline, bringing people to church so they could be added to the dehumanizing tally of "saved souls," thus affirming God's blessing on our congregation.

I did these things as best I could, oftentimes with enthusiasm. In spite of my twisted motivation and misguided theology, God still showed up. He's good like that.

When I failed to adhere to my strict religious and moral code, I tore myself down for not being stronger. Shame motivated me for a good year. But, of course, shame never sustains long-term change, and eventually I got tired of feeling like I couldn't measure up, so I quietly left the church and in a sense quit trying. Looking back now, leaving was probably a good thing.

I was so enslaved to being religious and trying to earn God's approval that I was unable to hear the Good News of Jesus Christ: God *loves* me. It's weird to think that my well-intentioned religious efforts managed to keep me away from God. Today I'm thankful I wasn't able to measure up to the standards I had placed on myself. Failure forced me to come to terms with the fact that I am in need. Weakness creates space for God. The healthy don't need a doctor.

I've come to feel sorry for people who form their identity based on their good works. If they fail, it only reinforces the self-disdain. And if they succeed, they have no use for God, like the Pharisees of Jesus's day, remaining contently engulfed in a world of rules where God is neatly packaged into formulas and clever acronyms, effectively suffocating mystery and grace.

Twenty years ago I first heard Brennan Manning talk of God's unconditional love for me, right here and right now, not as I should be but as I am. It was like a warm blanket covering a chill I didn't know I had. Out of his own brokenness, with a passion and tenderness I had never heard from a pulpit, Brennan said that God wasn't mad, that he just might have expected worse from me, that he aches for me to come home and crawl up into his arms of total acceptance and love and rest, that I couldn't wear out God's love, that there was nothing I could do to keep God from loving me, and that he was gentle and, unlike the world, never pushy or manipulative.

This began the slow death of my shame and guilt-ridden striving, launching what I assume will amount to a lifelong journey of learning and living as a child of God, loved beyond my comprehension.

"God, what do you think about me?" That was the little self-centered question I kept asking. Once I created enough space in the noise of my life to listen, God answered. In the following years of lonely retreats and long walks and bike rides, my soul began to be bathed in his love. Paradoxically, sometimes the silence brought boredom and sadness; other times I was just left sleepy and empty. A couple of times, I even waited curled in the fetal position, tugging my hair and sobbing. Yet through the years I occasionally entered into the holy hush of God's love, and through the air drifted the whisper of the most beautiful words:

> Oh, little one, there you are—don't run.
> Rest.
> It's okay to rest.
> You don't have to always keep going.
> I am already impressed.
>
> Remember I am for you.
> I have always been.
> I see how hard you try, how beat-up you feel, your mix
>   of motives and lost dreams.
>
> Just when you think you can't get any lower, I am there.
> Underneath your sadness and below the darkness of
>   your heart, I am there.

64

Your bottom is my beginning.
When you hurt, I hurt,
and when you open your heart to love, I stand up and
applaud.

As the years rolled by, I kept returning to the silence. I kept asking, and I began to form my identity around the answer.

I started seeing glimpses of God's unconditional love all around me.

I slowly stopped viewing the Bible as a book I needed to understand, manage, or defend, and I started cultivating a deep appreciation for it as the personal stories of a loving Father reaching out to his children. When I moved beyond the cultural nuances, it unfolded as a divinely inspired and often tragic story of love.

I also began to see the created order as God's first great book. Nature is the only book many throughout history have been exposed to. It is a beautiful tapestry declaring the mystery, goodness, and love of God. Reading such a detailed and rich text seems to require only silence and prayerful listening.

I dug deeper and uncovered God's love echoed in the writings and experiences of two thousand years of faithful Christ followers. I discovered the words of Jean Pierre de Caussaude: "The doctrine of pure love can only be learnt by God's action, not by any effort of our own spirit."[2] And I came to cherish the wisdom of Julian of Norwich: "God loved us before he made us; and his love has never diminished and never shall."[3]

I realized I had been asking the wrong questions about the prodigal son. I believe that if he left he would be welcomed back again and again. I began to understand that if the prodigal son knew the grace, love, and acceptance of his father, he would never want to leave.

I'm really leery when anyone says they have a singular, simple solution to life's problems, but I have continually found that a clear and deep knowing of God's love for me has been the key remedy I needed to untangle many of the problems I faced. Whether it was resentments, guilt, relational conflict, obsessive or controlling behaviors, people pleasing, greed, lust, withdrawing, negative self-talk, anger, or trying to find my identity in what I did or in other people, these were all at least in part rooted in my desire and striving to be significant—to be loved.

Through the years, when I felt my actions didn't measure up or I struggled with sin, I found myself greeting my failures with a gentle smile. I didn't have to achieve or be perfect. I am loved. Contrary to what I had previously thought, reckless grace didn't make me complacent. Being accepted just as I am motivated me to give and to love. When I realized I didn't have to strive, I found I wanted to.

People who know they are deeply loved by God are free to engage reality. People who know they are deeply loved by God freely love others.

Grace. Unconditional love. Acceptance. These truths are often absent from the composition of our communities, religious or not.

Much could be said on this topic, and many others have articulated it better than I can, but I have come to believe that God's love is the central message of Christianity, that living the kingdom life must be born out of an active response to a deep knowing of one's place as a much-loved daughter or son of the Author of Life.

I'm accepted. I'm loved. I'm free to achieve and to fail. I don't have to prove I'm worthy of love or forgiveness. And so it is out of this center that I now approach the spiritual disciplines.

I guess I agree with what I flippantly spouted to that mysterious lady: "If the spiritual life doesn't lead us to freedom and grace, then we've probably missed the point."

Understanding
Solitude

In our day God is using the spiritual discipline of solitude as the great liberator. Solitude liberates us from all the inane chatter that is so characteristic of modern life. It liberates us from the ever-present demands that are put upon us; demands that in the moment feel so urgent and pressing but that in reality have no lasting significance. In solitude the useless trivialities of life begin to drop away. We are set free from the many "false selves" we have built up in order to cope with the expectations others place upon us—and we place upon ourselves. Solitude empowers us to walk away from all human pretense and manipulation.

In addition, God uses our experiences of solitude to enable us to become who we truly are. We begin, slowly at first, to live simply before God. Increasingly we come to see things in the light of eternity, and as a result, successes and failures no longer impress us or oppress us. Experiences of solitude root in us a deep, abiding hope; a hope that sees everything in the light of God's overriding governance for good. In solitude we are so bathed in God's greatness and goodness that we come to see the immense value of our own soul. The result is that we become increasingly freed from our frantic human strivings.

Of course, all of our experiences in solitude are done in the presence of the living God. We are, after all, experiencing solitude as a Christian spiritual discipline. In times of solitude, we become enveloped in God's very presence.

There is an intimate connection between solitude and silence. Silence, you see, creates in us an open, empty space where we are enabled to become attentive to God. And oh, how we need such open spaces in our modern techno-world with its relentless barrage of "sound and fury, signifying nothing." Indeed, many people today have become little more than walking "towers of babble."

Today silence is one of the most essential disciplines of the Spirit simply because it puts a stopper on all this mindless chatter and clatter. It enables us to step aside from the noise and hurry and crowds of modern life long enough to allow God to create in us attitudes and habits that will hold us constantly in the loving presence of God.

There was a time, not so very long ago, when solitude and silence were available to people by the normal conditions of everyday life. Not any longer! In our day we have to *choose* solitude and silence and plan our lives accordingly. It can be done, of course, especially as we catch a vision of their liberating qualities. Thomas Merton wrote, "It is in deep solitude that I find the gentleness with which I can truly love [others]. . . . Solitude and silence teach me to love [others] for what they are, not for what they say."[1]

Richard J. Foster

Solitude

Souvenirs from the Void

The heart breaks and breaks and lives by breaking. It is necessary to go through dark and deeper dark and not to turn.

Stanley Kunitz[1]

Extroverts gain energy from being around people. Introverts gain energy from being alone. In the past I would have described myself as an extreme introvert. I fiercely craved solitude. This wasn't much of an issue when I was single or before having kids, but as I got older that desire became a huge problem. I worked directly with people all day, and at home my wife was waiting eagerly to talk to another adult and have a break from the kids, who also wanted nothing more than my undivided attention. To make matters worse, we lacked family or friends who could take the kids for more than the occasional break. Once we went an entire year without a date, and we went ten years with only one night away from parenting responsibilities.

While I loved my work and was thankful to live with people who liked me, I was dangerously taxed emotionally and mentally.

Going out to eat or seeing a movie alone were some of my favorite activities. I was often lost in daydreaming about an upcoming solo retreat or backpacking trip. Some people fantasize about having an affair; I fantasized about being a mountain hermit.

Learning to adapt to family life and working with people has been a painstaking process, but I'm happy to say I have done it. Although I'm still an introvert, I no longer need solitude in the same way I used to. I'm infatuated with my wife, and my kids are a joy to be around. At the end of the day, I can't wait to hang out with my family. I still need space alone, but being around people doesn't drain me in quite the same way it did. Yet changes, good or bad, always bring new challenges.

I'm now frightened of prolonged solitude.

I probably would have put off this discipline until the end had I not been invited to attend a writer's retreat that I really wanted to be a part of. Solitude was about to find me. It was beginning to seem like this was the case with the disciplines: as much as I was seeking them, specific opportunities to practice each one seemed to make a timely arrival. As the Buddhist proverb says, "When the student is ready, the teacher appears."

It's difficult to express just how worn and haggard I was when I traced the Virginia mountain back roads following cryptic directions to a retreat house. So much for my planned late-night escapes to the coffee shop in town; there was no town. I parked the car and began a hesitant march into the empty and lonely void of silence.

Slowly I creaked open a giant stained glass door and crossed the threshold into my personal abyss. With overwhelming enthusiasm and joy, my jailer, Ann, welcomed me into her scenic wooden cathedral and asked to wash my feet. Something happened when the warm water gurgled over my labored toes into a handcrafted pottery basin. A gentle hush of the Holy Spirit overtook me, and I could hardly speak. I hadn't felt God's presence like that in years. I hadn't rested in years. My retreat began.

I was given an exquisite room, a meal, and instructions to spend the next day in silence. I wanted to follow the rules. I wanted to get the full experience. But I cheated. I had met a couple of really interesting people and couldn't resist staying up late talking. I awoke determined to be silent.

I've heard people describe eating a meal with others in silence as a special spiritual experience. That morning, breakfast was just awkward. I felt like a little kid in the backseat of the car, forbidden to talk. I acted pretty much the same as I did when I was nine, smirking and making faces at my friend. I knew I had gone too far when I received a stern smile from one of the "more spiritual" people after I casually threw something at my new friend and we burst out laughing. It was time to quit playing around and dive into the silence.

With nothing but a book in tow, I wandered up a freshly cut path through waist-high grass. I was actually kind of excited to spend the entire day reorienting myself with my lost love, silence. I sat perched upon a treeless hill surrounded by a panoramic view of the gently sloping Blue Ridge Mountains. A refreshing cool summer breeze sliced through the humid air as the long grass danced across my earthen mound. I breathed in my surroundings and whispered a few prayers of gratitude.

Despite my setting, within fifteen minutes restlessness began to creep in. I spent the next half hour vacillating between pacing and leafing through my book. Then with unexpected force I was struck with suffocating emptiness. My heart raced. My palms perspired. It was the same darkness I had found while fasting. I quickly looked for a remedy. I had no phone, computer, TV, music, or person I could run to. I felt naked and alone.

"Shh, be still, child . . ." echoed a voice in my head. With the voice came a new courage. It was time to embrace whatever this madness was. It was time to face the beast, jump off the high dive, and run toward my fears.

Instantly I rose up and let out a tribal scream, then sprinted down the path. The trail went up and down, following a broad ridge that soon narrowed as the grass tightened around me. Slowing my pace, I stretched my arms out wide and stroked the grass. I glided up a ridge to a dead end at a beautifully constructed rock structure. I fell to my knees and began sobbing.

I lay prostrate at the end, carelessly resting my tear-stained cheek against the earth. I didn't want to continue. I couldn't continue.

I'm not entirely sure what transpired in the next hour, and the full extent of some stories are best left untold, but in short, it was a sort of facing and acceptance of what Freudians term our death wish. It's not that I really wanted to die—my life is good and I want to be around for my wife and kids—but for years I have sort of felt done with living. Strange as it sounds, much of this coincided with watching my goals and dreams come true. For the most part I was where I wanted to be in life. My mountains had all been climbed. Achievement comes with its own challenges, and ironically, it marked a sort of end to my drive and motivation for life. What more does this world have to offer? Career? Money? Experiences? Fun and novel as these things sound, they're also sort of empty. I get tired of trying to navigate life. Going home to be with God sometimes feels more appealing than what this world has to offer. The words of Solomon often echo in my head: "I have seen all the things that are done under the sun; all of them are meaningless, a chasing after the wind."[2]

I hope you won't find it too dramatic if I tell you I found purpose and meaning for my life while rolling in dirt and grass and sobbing at the end of a trail. I half wish I could say that I came out of the experience with a grand vision for founding a ministry to end world hunger and oppression, or that I had a prophetic word that I should keep plucking at the bass because the band I was forming with my wife was about to launch us into crazy music stardom. But if you define grand as spending my time and energy focusing on loving those around me—family, friends, and students—then yes, I left with a grand vision. It's not that I previously didn't understand the importance of these aspects of life, but something shifted in the way I was seeing how to live in the kingdom—here and now.

I was overcome with a profound realization that spending this season of my life doing things that are simple, local, and relatively hidden, growing in love for God and others, is the highest and noblest goal I could now achieve. And so when I'm finished here on earth, nothing better could be written on my tombstone than:

Here lies Nate.
He loved well.

Finding motivation to embrace the years ahead was an invaluable gift the solitude brought me, a souvenir of sorts. But the day wasn't over.

Later that afternoon as I was sitting alone in the woods, a magnitude 5.8 earthquake shook the east coast. Apparently, I was thirty miles from the epicenter and the retreat house bent and buckled from the blast. Two hundred miles away, the Pentagon and White House were evacuated. Strangely, I felt nothing. In my quiet solitude, the only shift I noticed was a lone leaf on a newly sprouted tree violently quivering. It's not that I was sleeping or lost in some trance. I was watching and listening to the forest, studying and enjoying every sound and movement, but for some reason, the earth around me remained solid.

I composed a sort of psalm about the experience:

Let the earth shake
Grab the seams and turn 'em loose
Let the temples fall
Bring down our vain attempts at divinity

For in your gentle embrace I will rest
In your care, the chaos and clamor is but a quivering
leaf.

As I flew home, nature's wildness wasn't done teaching. A lightning storm shut down the Detroit airport, and my flight had to land in Ohio. After one particularly rough patch of turbulence, the man next to me was so frightened he screamed, throwing in a few choice words.

I closed my eyes and let my mind wander. *What strange irony. I don't want to go, my tombstone has yet to be written! I want to live!* I pictured the quivery leaf. I smiled and whispered,

Let the plane twist and shake.
God is in control.
I can rest in his gentle embrace;
the chaos and clamor of life is but a quivering leaf.

As I sleepily wandered down the 2:00 a.m. barren highway toward home, I reflected on this special trip. I've only had a couple of experiences this significant in my lifetime and don't expect to have many more. That four-day retreat was a blend of rest, silence, mystery, and wonderful conversation with new friends. I laughed, I listened, I prayed. Above all, I ingested stillness. Joy was creeping into the shadows.

The following morning, I was exceptionally eager to see my family. I felt like a different person, with a new stillness and mission. Sometimes kids make me nervous; there's something about their wild energy that intimidates me. They're so free that you never really know what they're going to do next. The contrast between the stillness I carried back from the woods and the untamed energy of my son climbing, jumping, and pulling on me while my daughter was giving me a detailed account of everything she had done, read, and watched while I was gone was just too much. Almost immediately I felt my patience wearing. Within two hours I overreacted and in a loud voice scolded my son. He ran to his room in tears.

"They're just excited to see you. Calm down," my wife, Christy, implored. With demoralized frustration, I retreated to my office and sulked.

What was wrong with me? After a four-day break filled with such wonder, I couldn't even handle a couple hours of parenting? It was almost as if I was worse for having rested, or at least that's how it felt. I had lost the rhythm of handling my life.

I was ready to forget my epitaph. I just wasn't up for the task of loving well.

Solitude
Anthony of the Desert (250–356)

Anthony of the Desert (also known as Anthony the Great, Saint Anthony, Anthony of Egypt, or Abba Anthony) is the most well known of the desert fathers. The desert fathers were Christian hermits and are thought to have been the first Christian monks, with Anthony being considered the father of monasticism.

Anthony was born into a wealthy family. When he was twenty, both of his parents died, leaving him with a vast inheritance. However, upon hearing Matthew 19:21, Anthony took literally Jesus's calling to give all possessions to the poor and follow Christ. Anthony initially moved to the outskirts of town, but as word spread of his wisdom and the healings people experienced through him, he gradually retreated farther into the desert for fear of becoming prideful and of people worshiping him instead of God. At one point he even lived in a secluded room for twenty years, relying on his friends to bring him bread.

Of solitude he is known to have said, "Just as fish die if they stay too long out of water, so the monks who loiter outside their cells or pass their time with men of the world lose the intensity of inner peace. So like a fish going towards the sea, we must hurry to reach our cell, for fear if we delay outside we will lose our interior watchfulness."[3]

Saint Anthony strived to "live a life of continual sacrifice" as an alternative type of martyrdom. He lived healthily to the age of 105. Even in death he chose humility by being buried in an unknown location instead of having his body mummified and displayed in a place of honor, as was the practice in Egypt.

Understanding
Meditation

Prayer is the interactive relationship we have with God about what we and God are working on together. Christian meditation is the listening side of this interactive relationship. God speaks and teaches; we hear and obey. To use the graphic phrase of Dallas Willard, God is "our communicating cosmos."

God uses various and sundry means for speaking and teaching. God speaks to us through the book of Scripture, the Bible. God speaks to us through the "book" of nature. God speaks to us through the action and activity of the Holy Spirit. God speaks to us directly, heart to heart. God's "still small voice" can indeed be heard and understood.

Jesus reminds us that he is the Good Shepherd and that his sheep know his voice. Jesus Christ is alive and here to teach his people himself. His voice is not hard to hear; his vocabulary is not difficult to understand. Meditation is *the* spiritual discipline that helps us to listen well and to hear correctly.

At its most basic and fundamental level, Christian meditation is simply a loving attentiveness to God. Through the prophet Isaiah, God urges us to "Incline your ear, and come to me; listen, so that you may live."[1] Listening is the key. Hear the life-giving counsel of Francois Fenelon: "Be silent, and listen to God. Let your heart be in such a state of preparation that his Spirit may impress upon you such virtues as will please him. Let all within you listen to him. This silence of all outward and earthly affection and of human thoughts within us is essential if we are to hear his voice."[2]

Through meditation we are growing into what Thomas à Kempis called "a familiar friendship with Jesus." We are creating the emotional and spiritual space that allows God to construct within us an inner sanctuary of the heart. Here, in this inner sanctuary, we learn to listen to God, "in his wondrous, terrible, gentle, loving, all-embracing silence," as Catherine de Hueck Doherty put it.[3]

In Revelation 3:20 we are given the wonderful words of Jesus, "Listen! I am standing at the door, knocking; if you hear my voice and open the door, I will come in to you and eat with you, and you with me." These words were originally penned for believers, not unbelievers. You see, Jesus is knocking at the door of your heart and my heart. He is longing to eat with us, to commune with us. He desires a perpetual eucharistic feast in the inner sanctuary of the heart. Jesus is knocking; meditative prayer opens the door.

The wise old apostle Paul reminds us that God is gathering to himself an all-inclusive community of loving persons, "a holy temple in the Lord; in whom you also are built together spiritually into a dwelling place for God."[4] This is staggering news! We, individually and together, are becoming "a dwelling place for God." The Christian spiritual discipline of meditation prepares the way.

Richard J. Foster

Meditation

Cooking Chemicals in My Head

Nothing in all creation is so like God as silence.

Meister Eckhart[1]

My commute to work is ten miles by bike on a wooded path. Steadying my cadence, I pound out the first few miles while a confident breeze begins its arduous process of ripping the stress and worries from my scattered mind. Somewhere between mile two and mile four, I stop asking why I didn't drive or wear warmer clothes, and I melt into the hum of my tires gently caressing the earth. It is here that God's great book of nature weaves a kind of magic, and the remaining miles often become a mix of birthed ideas, untangled problems, and chapters I intend to write.

An array of wildlife joins me on my commuting adventure. I've seen turtles, frogs, beavers, cats, muskrat, foxes, marmots, mice, and even a few snakes. I can count on hearing birds chirping about and watching the occasional eagle or hawk gliding above. There are always deer. Because I want to be like Saint

Francis, I talk and sing to my deer; I even slow down to give space for their reply. They only respond with fear and gallop away.

Of all the wonders the trail offers, it's the subtle shift of the seasons that most captivates me; no two days are alike. As it is in life, change is always brewing. Nature's quiet brutality is on full display during a Michigan winter. The ground is covered with snow for all but a handful of days, while the sun sleeps behind the clouds. Life is a blurry mix of cold and gray. The angst and sadness of winter are what first drove me outdoors to exercise. Running or biking in a blizzard was my way of declaring independence from winter's spell. Winter doesn't have to own me; circumstances don't always have to dictate my life. My body can adapt. Part of what drives young men off to war drives me into the cruel cold. With snow tires intact, biking in the winter addresses my frustration at living the life of an emasculated male working at a desk.

During winter, nature is busy. Trees do most of their growing as roots search deep, plumbing the earth in search of nutrients. In a season that seems dormant and asleep, God is active. These are good metaphors for spiritual formation.

As harsh as Michigan's winter is, its spring is equally glorious. Sure, green covers most of the country a good month before it reaches Michigan, but nowhere except up north does such enchantment permeate the air when winter's cruel curse is released. Down every street, herds of resurrected people emerge from their homes. Cheerfully they rake fall's leftover moldy leaves, plant bulbs, go for walks, and play. Frost subsiding is a truly communal form of awakening—one of the few I've experienced. The older deer, with their winter-battered coats, walk with a sense of pride. It won't be long until they're able to parade their delicately spotted young. The fruit of winter's labor will soon be on full display.

In the midst of early summer bike rides, my own personal winter had begun: a debilitated knee and extreme back pain.

I would spend a week confined to bed and over a month off of the bike. It would be fall before I would be able to handle the twenty-mile round-trip to work again.

When I'm riddled with debilitating anxiety, the occasional depressive spell, or the normal chaos of life, managing work and family feels unbearable and exercise is my main treatment. It's a medicine that I have become dependent upon in order to function in life. My therapist says exercise is a way of cooking chemicals in my head that have a sedating effect; to some extent I think she's right. Exercise is a natural way for my body to regulate mood. Having my ability to exercise taken away was, in a sense, similar to a horse being denied a pasture. At least it felt that way.

In excruciating pain, I lay in bed jealously watching my community come alive on a pristine 70-degree day. In my suffering and disappointment, I planted frustration. Self-pity nurtured and watered it; soon it was budding with anger, and within days bitterness was in full bloom. Bitterness, of course, effectively functions as a poison that soon bleeds onto everyone around. I was irritable.

In the middle of an argument, my insightful wife suggested that it might be time to work on the discipline of meditation. I quickly explained that she obviously didn't understand my situation. Gracefully she reminded me that a lot of people were in hospital beds begging God to have what I had.

Ouch.

After the sting of my pride subsided, I decided to give meditation a try.

In silence I gently turned my attention away from my self-pity and toward God. I let my barrage of thoughts drift by. I breathed, and I listened. After some time, my mind shifted to my current predicament, and a smile burst forth. I found myself reminded of God's uncanny ability to make good out of bad and that love calls me to grow, die to self, and suffer well. Soon

I was overcome with calm. My edges were softened. Life felt workable.

Reinhold Niebuhr said it well in the seldom-quoted second half of his famous Serenity Prayer:

> Living one day at a time,
> Enjoying one moment at a time,
> Accepting hardship as the pathway to peace.
> Taking, as Jesus did, this sinful world as it is,
> Not as I would have it.
> Trusting that He will make all things right
> if I surrender to His will.
> That I may be reasonably happy in this life,
> And supremely happy with Him forever in the next.[2]

Within days I found that meditation filled the mental void that my injuries had left. Meditation seemed to mirror my experiences exercising. For years I had seen the bike not as a way to improve my physique, although that was a nice benefit, but rather as a way to reset my head; a mental reboot of sorts. When I walked out the door to bike, hike, run, or swim, this was my chance to grab a few moments of solitude. It was a time for quiet reflection and an opportunity to still my soul. Was the aspect of biking I felt that I needed the meditative part? Does meditation also cook chemicals in my brain?

As I lay in bed quietly reflecting, it came as a bit of a shock to see that in commuting to work over the years, I had actually unintentionally been practicing meditation. I thought the disciplines required intentionality! Even more confusing was the realization that it wasn't just meditation I practiced when I exercised. I would inadvertently flow between other spiritual disciplines as well. For example, my exercise of choice almost always involved nature. The woods are alive, a thoughtful blend of beauty, wildness, mystery, and wonder instinctively obeying the will of the Father. I find it difficult to be immersed in the creative order and not spontaneously worship its Author and Sustainer.

As my soul and mind ease, worship often turns to prayer, usually without words but with gentle nudges of my soul. The wannabe artist in me paints a portrait with prayer, intently listening to God's direction, creating images and movements in my imagination. I don't usually pray the traditional catalogue-of-desires type of prayer; rather I throw out ideas or concerns and allow God space to respond, nudge, and guide.

As I continued to think about my time on the bike, I realized attaching note cards to my handlebars and slowly working on the discipline of study had become a habit. In spite of my challenges with actually memorizing the lines, I wondered if the repetitive movement of my body was a form of kinetic learning and I was laying down the new neural pathways.

Sometimes I was just quiet and listened. While my time out on the bike was usually fairly brief, it was in fact a great way to sample solitude as well. Especially if I was able to go places void of the commercial and cement distractions that seem to pervade our landscape.

Of course, my riding doesn't always have a spiritual element. Sometimes I blare music from my phone or hammer the pedals until I'm breathless. However, I wonder if fun and excitement don't also hold a flavor of the holy.

I'm not sure how I had missed the spiritual aspects of my exercise, but before being injured I was largely unaware of how integral exercise was in the formation of my soul. Maybe I'm not such a slacker in my spiritual life after all. Could it be that a few little habits had become ingrained and were now an instinctive part of my times of exercise? I think the fact that I enjoyed these times threw me off. So far during this project I had found an ease and joy in practicing the disciplines, at least for the most part. But I was still under the impression that they were supposed to have at least some element of drudgery. Maybe that would come later.

It was time to give my dad a call. He was always eager to hear about my project.

"Dad, when practicing meditation, I seem to seamlessly shift to other disciplines."

He responded like a good spiritual director and began laughing again. "Yeah, I know. They almost always lead into each other. In a sense the categories are artificial. One discipline almost always moves into another. You're on the right track."

"Okay, good. But what about intentionality?" I explained my experience on the bike and how I did the disciplines without really trying.

"Many things are happening unconsciously in life," he said. "We don't always realize what's going on until later. One of the fun things about teaching the spiritual disciplines is that it helps people realize what they're already doing. They become more conscious about times of training and easily add new practices to their life.

"But," he continued, "more important than how frequently or intensely we practice the disciplines is that our intention is to always be available to God. You know, you can pray more and become worse for it. Just look at the Pharisees, arrogant and rigid. Religion gone bad is worse than just about anything. The moment the disciplines become an end in themselves—they have failed."

"You mean it's kind of like the difference between the greased-up muscle guys at my gym who stare at themselves in the mirror and the older lady who takes a walk every day?" I ventured. "They are both doing exercises, but one is doing it for vanity and the other so she can stay healthy and live to see her granddaughter get married."

"You got it, Nate. The athletic metaphor is a good one. Think of the older lady who works hard with the intention of maintaining good health. I bet she has developed other healthy habits unintentionally, like taking the stairs or walking to the grocery store. Good health is a natural part of her life. She has developed ingrained habits, so it's not necessarily something she thinks about. It's the same in the spiritual life. It's good you are doing things you're not aware of, Nate. It means it's starting to stick."

"Well, all right. It's hard not to get caught up in thinking maybe I should be trying harder. So far this process has been relatively easy. Aren't the disciplines supposed to hold more drudgery?"

Shifting to his teaching voice, Dad continued with passion, reciting phrases I'm sure he's uttered hundreds of times. "You're thinking of rigidity—that's not discipline. People confuse the two. Virtue is easy; it's vice that's hard. Remember, virtue is good habits you can rely on to make your life work. Vice is bad habits you can rely on to make your life not work—dysfunction."

I knew about vice, and while I agreed it had a tendency to make life miserable, it seemed so easy to fall into. Trying to live a virtuous life had been a great struggle for me, at least at first. But I had learned through the years that things just seem to go better when I make good choices. So much of my misery in life was of my own doing, born from my choices or the negative reactions I'd had to others' actions. I was reminded of a statement my daughter had shared with me that she adapted from a Martin Luther King Jr. quote: "I decided to choose love; hate is too big of a burden to bear."[3] Maybe virtue *was* the easier path.

🌳🌳🌳

Many meditative techniques have been developed by a variety of religious and nonreligious traditions. The main distinction of Christian meditation is a focus on filling rather than emptying. It is not done as a self-help mechanism or a tool to relax, although it almost always results in relaxation, but rather as a way to connect with God, to hear and obey. Christians throughout the centuries have followed biblical examples of meditation in a variety of ways that people find helpful to the process: sitting in silence before God, focusing on a verse or picture, spending time in nature, using music or various imaginative exercises. Christian meditation, sometimes referenced as contemplative or meditative prayer, is essentially little more than an active response to the verse, "Be still, and know that I am God."[4] It is a time to discern the "still small voice" of Yahweh.[5]

It wasn't until I began to formally study Christian meditation that I realized this has been the primary activity I have used through the years to encounter God.

Since there are forty-two biblical references to meditation, it's odd how absent the practice is from modern Western Christianity. For many Christians, meditation is often seen as a practice reserved for New Age or Middle Eastern religions, and many are unaware of its deep roots in historic Christian practice and thought. Not to mention that stillness is an affront to our idols of efficiency, hurry, noise, and distraction. Spirituality with no concretely defined goals and objectives can be threatening. We almost always value purpose over mystery.

Some Christians go so far as to object to the practice altogether for fear that using one's imagination is a gateway to the demonic. How many good things do fear and misunderstanding keep us from? The human imagination is an amazing God-given gift. Our world is full of examples of its redemptive use—art, music, and innovations.

⁂

For me, meditation usually begins with closing my eyes and taking a series of deep breaths. This helps me begin to let go of the distractions and temporal concerns that seem to dominate much of my life. Some thoughts I let drift by; others that I need to remember I jot down. I prayerfully invite God to guide my time while I simply focus my attention on him. Oftentimes I silently pray, confess, worship, untangle situations, and make resolutions. Sometimes I just sit and listen. Occasionally, I fall asleep. I don't think God minds; he knows when I'm exhausted and mean well.

In special moments the silence of meditation ushers in wonder and joy. As I'm carried into the mystery of God, the stillness is like breast milk from God: tender, loving, and intimate.

Often, however, silence brings emptiness. I get to face the emotion that seems most characteristic of the human experience: loneliness. I'm reminded of how I tend to turn good things like family, friends, social media, work, church activities, sex, TV, books, internet, future goals, spending money, sports, and hobbies into distractions in order to fill the void.

In the depths of meditation, I sometimes well up in tears. I'm aware I don't know how to live, how to be. I become more in touch with my body, my heart, my surroundings. It is not escapism; it is becoming alive to the world, alive to the presence of God in his created order.

Boredom is the key. You know you're getting close when you begin to feel its empty weight. Monotony ushers in joy. I realize how seldom I fully enjoy the richness of the sacred. I'm frightened by how distracted my life has become. I used to think multitasking was a virtue to strive for. It is not. The forgotten art of focusing on one task at a time is a treasure, a joy, and the gateway to a life of prayer. In this space we learn to listen. We gently respond to the rhythms of the Spirit.

While physical, mental, and innate awareness of God's presence or voice is one of the most glorious things a human can experience, his hiddenness is as much an act of love as his presence. Like the tree digging its roots deep in the earth, desperately searching for the water it needs to survive, we pursue God in spite of what we experience or feel. God's seeming absence is vital for the growth of our souls. Spiritual maturity requires both presence and longing.

With over two thousand years of Christendom to draw from, there is a long legacy of books written by Jesus followers to lead and guide us. I'm not sure if we are facing a decaying spiritual evolution or if I'm just a book snob, but it seems the most substantial books, the type of book that can only be written after collecting a lifetime of knowledge and experience, are older. Modern books often lack the bite, depth, and courage of the old writers.

Years ago, when I was first introduced to the idea of sitting in God's presence, a good five minutes was about all I could handle. Here again I have had to let go of my obsession with progress. While I haven't intentionally meditated with regularity, it has quietly become a major part of my life. And it's only after years of practice that I can now sit for extended periods of time. Yet I find it doesn't take long to reset my attention to the work of the Spirit brooding and hovering about, pursuing and loving his creation. So when I find a moment or two, I welcome God's presence and find, as Henri Nouwen said, "The inner fire of God is tended and kept alive."[6]

My days injured in bed gave me plenty of space for reading and thinking. I realized I need to actively reintroduce meditation into my life beyond my time biking. Much like I need to drink water, I have to keep going back to the source throughout the day. Taking short breaks to meditate, even for five minutes, seemed to propel me to deal with the creative, inspiring, life-giving energy from my kids that can sometimes feel so overwhelming. While I want my motivation for seeking God to be pure and free of selfish desires, in truth, meditation, as well as other disciplines, is turning out to be very useful. The results exceed my efforts.

In the weeks and months to come, I found it wasn't necessary to run away for days of solitude to find God's gentle presence. I could hold a meditative awareness of him in the midst of the crowds and the noise of life. God seemed ever happy to find me in the middle of wherever I was. How scandalous of him to be so practical.

Is a consistent practice of meditation what I need to meet my goal of loving others extravagantly? At least for now, attention on God's presence in my interactions with others brings a calm that helps me engage and show up for life in the midst of the stress and chaos that seem so prevalent. I just might get to become the dad, husband, teacher, and friend I want to be after all—one who loves well.

By fall I was back on my bike, although I didn't return with the same fervor but rather with gentleness in both body and mind. However, the wind continued to foretell yet another change. The leaves prepared for death, revealing their glory, shown bright and dull, yellow and orange. An occasional tree was bold enough to display a red as rich as blood. Patiently they waited for just the right moment, and then, one by one, they answered the call of the wind and leaped into the air, their first and only great flight. I watched their ballet as they dove to their deaths with freedom and grace. Soon they would decay, their energy seeping into the ground, providing the rich nutrients necessary for the forest life to live on. Life from death. Even creation resonates the Jesus narrative.

A Portrait of

Meditation
Thomas Merton (1915–1968)

Originally from France, Merton studied English literature at Clare College in Cambridge and Columbia University in New York. He converted to Roman Catholicism in 1938.

By 1941, Merton became a Trappist monk and lived at the Gethsemani abbey in Kentucky. In 1948, Merton penned one of the most significant Christian autobiographies of the twentieth century, *The Seven Storey Mountain*. This work tells of his conversion experience and presents a compelling argument to Western Christians for spiritual monasticism.

Merton took the example of the desert fathers and Saint John of the Cross and presented this monastic life in a way that is palatable to Western Christians. The meditative, contemplative, solitude-filled life was not a spiritual walk reserved only for hermits but one applicable and necessary for all Christians. He often sought out nature and silence as the ideal setting in which to meditate. Merton often referred to the act of meditation as "listening prayer." He thought meditation should be a daily act and we should avoid reflecting on anything specifically but simply relax in the presence of God.

Merton was open to interfaith dialogue and was very interested in the meditative and contemplative practices of non–Roman Catholic and even non-Christian traditions. Tragically, Merton's life ended in 1968 when he was accidentally electrocuted by a fan while stepping out of a bath.

Understanding
Confession

Confession is the spiritual discipline that allows us to enter into the grace and mercy of God in such a way that we experience forgiveness and healing for the sins and sorrows of the past.

Both forgiveness and healing are involved in confession. Forgiveness positions us in a right relationship toward God—objective righteousness, to use a theological term. Healing frees us from the domination of our present by our past—subjective righteousness, to use another term from theology.

It is the cross of Jesus Christ that makes both the forgiveness and the healing a reality. Without the cross, the discipline of confession would be only psychologically therapeutic.

The redemptive process of the cross of Christ is a great mystery hidden in the heart of God. Sophisticated theories have been devised to help us better understand what happened on the cross—ransom theory, satisfaction theory, substitutionary theory, moral influence theory, and more. The Canons of Dort summarize the matter this way: "The death of the Son of God is the only and most perfect sacrifice and satisfaction for sins, of infinite value and worth, abundantly sufficient to expiate the sins of the whole world." These explanations do help us in some measure. But the mystery remains.

Here is what we do know: Jesus on the cross somehow took into himself all of the sin and all of the evil of all of humanity and redeemed it. Jesus, who had walked in constant communion with the Father, now on the cross became so totally identified with humankind that he was the actual embodiment of sin. Paul put it this way: "For our sake [God] made him to be sin who knew no sin, so that in him we might become the righteousness of God."[1] How all this transpired we do not understand, and perhaps at this point our understanding needs to give way to doxology.

Confession is both private and communal. It is a wonderful truth that the individual can break through into new life through the cross without the aid of any human mediator. But if we have not experienced release from the sins and sorrows of the past by means of private confession, we have not exhausted our resources, nor God's grace. In *The Book of Common Prayer* we read these encouraging words: "If there be any of you who by this means cannot quiet his own conscience herein but require further comfort or counsel, let him come to me or to some other minister of God's Word, and open his grief."

So God has given the Christian fellowship to help us. We can share our burden with another in the Christian community. Such persons will stand in Christ's stead and give us the word of forgiveness in Christ's name. "If we confess our sins, he who is faithful and just will forgive us our sins and cleanse us from all unrighteousness."[2]

Confession shows us the greatness and the goodness of God. Bernard of Clairvaux captures this reality well when he writes:

> To shame our sins He blushed in blood;
> He closed His eyes to show us God;
> Let all the world fall down and know
> That none but God such love can show.[3]

Richard J. Foster

Confession

My Redemption Tour

Confession is not an act to degrade yourself, but to
be set free.

Christy Foster

Submission and fasting forced me to examine my need for control. Study brought fortitude. In solitude and meditation I created space for God to speak. When I set aside noises and distractions, my heart reminds me of its treasures but also its losses. Echoes of past actions and hurts reverberate in the stillness. We cannot enter into silence without confession. I used to deny past hurts and their calls for liberation, thinking avoidance was an act of strength. But the cloud of regrets that imprisoned me had only one remedy: forgiveness. I have come to believe that few things require more bravery than facing ourselves and the messes we make in this life. Humans need the discipline of confession.

I was raised in a generation whose leaders didn't apologize. Strength meant you never said you were sorry, even if you were clearly wrong. All the great films when I was growing up were based on revenge. The power of a grudge could take an ordinary man and transform him into a brave fighting machine. The messages were always the same: forgiveness is weak; vengeance epitomizes masculine strength. Yet the life of Jesus stands in complete opposition to our cultural values.

So many of us only turn to confession and forgiveness when all else fails and it feels like an absolute necessity. I'm no stranger to the discipline of confession. I've told all my secrets.

A few years ago I worked through the Twelve Steps as outlined by Bill Wilson and Robert Smith in their book *Alcoholics Anonymous.*[1]

Step 4 was to make "a searching and fearless moral inventory."[2] Guided by my sponsor, I was given simple instructions. "Write down everything you have ever done wrong in your entire life. Be as thorough as possible. Leave nothing out." I've made enough bad choices to have made this a fairly arduous task, but the real pain was to come next.

Step 5: "admitted to God, to ourselves, and to another human being the exact nature of our wrongs."[3] My sponsor worked on coal mining equipment in rural Kentucky. When we needed extended time to talk, I would occasionally go along with him to work. Since the dawn of creation, few people have been deep in the Appalachian Mountains. Unless they're unearthing coal, people don't go to these forgotten places. The roads are dangerously winding and desolate. As his truck gently traced the curvy road, I read my list and told my stories. I went deep into the chasm of my life and mercilessly pulled loose everything hidden, exposing my darkness to daylight, laying it before God, myself, and another person. Later that afternoon I watched as miners emerged from their pit, exhausted, covered in soot, and happy to be free from the darkness. I felt the same.

Apparently, if you apply enough pressure to coal, this dark, dusty, energy-packed substance transforms into a diamond. I'm not sure I would say my mess has become a diamond, but I wouldn't have traded the feeling I had that afternoon for a whole bag.

It's not that I was really holding anything in; I had been in counseling for years. But there was something about putting it all out there at once. When my sponsor leaned over, briefly taking his eyes off the road, and in his thick Appalachian drawl whispered that I was forgiven, a tear rolled down my cheek and a smile burst forth. I felt free. Naked, exposed, accepted.

Few words are more powerfully disarming than "I'm sorry." Few words are more liberating than "I forgive you."

I've come to value making amends; it helps me sleep at night. I've watched it save friendships and forge my marriage.

🌲🌲🌲

I met Tim when we worked together in the Colorado Rockies at a residential treatment center for high-risk adolescents. It was a rough place to work; many burned out, including us. The treatment center had closed down a few years earlier, and Tim was now living in a house on the property. It had been ten years since I had written my last shift report, turned in my keys, and driven off with no intention of ever returning. Now I was back on a free afternoon during a speaking trip in Colorado, and despite my fear, I asked Tim if he would show me around the abandoned facility and be my confessional priest.

I'm sure he knew what had happened, but I wanted to tell my story in its entirety. So as we wandered the hills of this abandoned mountain camp, I relived it all. It had been my first job out of college. I was excited. I would spend my days working in the mountains, occasionally taking kids hiking and backpacking. Yet when I realized that I and one other person alone would be responsible for enforcing a strict labor-camp-style schedule on twenty unruly, abandoned, criminal boys, I was terrified. I wasn't entirely sure how I would implement required hours of hard labor, six-minute showers, and 5:30 a.m. wake-up calls, not to mention forcing teenage boys to wear an orange jumpsuit if they were seen as a run risk. The day of physical restraint training and the locked and padded room looming at the end of a dark hallway suggested how rules might be enforced. The other employees welcomed me with violent tales of mythological proportion; they laughed at the police's reluctance to make the thirty-minute drive to our isolated facility. With much fear and lots of prayer, I faced the challenge.

As it turned out, I wasn't entirely out of my element. I knew their games and their wounds; they were a lot like me and the people I hung around with growing up.

I went there to serve, to be helpful, and to do ministry. I did it all with great intensity. I prayed with the kids and cried with them. I took my share of punches and verbal abuse, and when things got really out of control, I wrestled them to the ground, where I and another staff member would pin them facedown, holding them until they relented. Sometimes the struggle could last for what seemed like an hour.

This was the hardest and most beautiful work I have ever done. I learned more in less than a year about the human experience, love, tenderness, strength, hope, and fear than I would at any other time in my life.

I wish I could say the worst part of the job was the stress, the violence, the time I punched my wife in the arm while asleep during a nightmare, or the six months of factory work I left there to do after vowing to never again work with people, but it wasn't.

Life is not perfect. We try. We succeed and we fail. We break things. Sometimes when we try to help, we end up causing damage.

As Tim and I crept through the dusty halls, we pointed out places and shared stories. We collected memories and processed that trying season. My heart raced nervously as the time had come to confess the worst. "You know, I did restraints that were unnecessary. I was scared. I had lost control and just didn't know what to do. I said things that were so demoralizing. I even spit at a kid once."

I'm not exactly sure what Tim said to me. He was a gracious listener and had his own stories of regret to tell. Truth is, our judgment had been so blurred and we knew it. Rather than leave, we joined in on a sick system driven by power and control.

After our tour was complete, we climbed up to a nearby mountain ledge and dangled our feet from the rocks, overlooking the wooded valley below.

"I should have left before it got that bad," I muttered.

"We all should have left." He chuckled.

"You know what, Tim? I had such rough teenage years. I made a mess of things. I hurt people. I half wonder if I came to work here as a way to pay penance for my wrongs."

After a thoughtful pause, Tim responded with gentle authority, "Well, maybe. You served your time. You can let it go, Nate . . . all of it!"

And so I did.

There was something about revisiting the place, inhabiting the space, soaking in the smells and feel that created an open space for confession. As I flew back to Michigan, it began to dawn on me that included in the speaking trips I had planned for the upcoming year were all five states I had ever lived in. Ah, the hand of providence. I decided to make more confessions. I decided this would be my "redemption tour."

When I first started this project, I created a list of all the interesting ways I planned to practice each discipline, but here again, the disciplines were finding me. It was as if all I had to do was tune my awareness to potential opportunities and they naturally presented themselves. I discarded my list and let go of my agenda for how to practice each discipline. God was guiding.

Oregon

As I sat listening to the chapel music play while I was waiting to speak, tears of gratitude rolled down my face. I stood up and told the crowd not to worry if they have failing grades and decide to leave the university to be a janitor and live in an RV, because they too just might get asked to come back and be a chapel speaker. Holding my book *Wisdom Chaser*[4] in hand, I said that even if they fail freshman English, one day they too might get to write a book.

I once heard it said that God takes us back to our places of failure to redeem us. This was certainly the case for me.

I made my confessions, forgave myself, and then climbed Mount St. Helens.

Kansas

His hobbit-hole office was at the end of a dark, narrow corridor, lined to the ceiling with obscure books and old religious art. Father Terry rocked in his worn chair and quietly peered into the shadowed distance. He gently stroked his twelve-inch silver goatee like it was a golden lamp capable of unleashing a genie to unlock the mystery and wisdom of the ages.

For the last twenty years, Terry had been my mentor. Together we talked deep into the night. Amidst updates and laughs, I casually made my Kansas confessions. In return he offered a strange, almost prophetic insight.

"Why did Jesus name the demons before he told them to leave? In the Hebrew tradition, when you named something, you took power over it." He cited a couple of biblical examples, including Adam and the animals and the strange story of Moses asking for God's name.

"Three times Moses asked! Finally God answered, 'I AM WHO I AM!'[5] In other words, I'll be what you need me to be. It was a response of intimacy, covenant, and in a sense, authority." The power in naming.

Father Terry calmly sat in silence, nursing steaming tea from a ceramic mug.

"It's the wonder of confession. Naming our sins takes back the power they once had over us," he casually tossed into the fire of thoughts.

"When I call it out, I'm no longer controlled by denial, secrets, or shame," I whispered into the dark.

Terry smiled.

I remain free to be just who God needs me to be, I thought.

"I am who I am" would become my new mantra.

⁂

My childhood wounds are nebulous, a bitter pureed soup of melancholy, unmet needs, and unrealistic desires seasoned with bad choices, false perceptions, and painful circumstances. While my growing-up years hold some good memories, the cracks and corners are laced with rejection and sadness. I no longer wonder what went wrong, who did or didn't do what; it's fruitless and nearly impossible to assign blame to the scars. I'm left to take responsibility for my own choices, both past and present. The Midwest image of dusty wind scouring the dry and foliageless prairie serves as the perfect metaphor for how I perceived my childhood.

I trembled as I parked the car at the end of the block and nervously sauntered down the street. I traced the lines in the pavement. I knew every crack and bump, having covered it on my bike and skateboard thousands of times. And there it was, the haunted house of Faulkner Avenue. It was you, reader, who pushed me up to the front door to ring the bell. I knew you'd want me to. I knew it would make a good story. Thank you.

At age sixteen I left this house with a haphazardly packed old canvas backpack and headed to Oregon. Later that summer my parents moved across town. Someone else packed up my room; someone else said good-bye; I never did.

For twenty years I'd moved those boxes that were packed for me from house to house. Many remained unpacked, rotting in my shed. I said I didn't have time to sort through them, but the truth is, it felt safe to have them hidden in darkness, closed and unnamed.

When I was a kid, I believed my room was haunted. Many nights I went to bed filled with terror as I watched shadowy figures scurry about, taunting me. Drug-induced hallucination? Demons summoned by my sins or the birth of a mental illness? I don't know.

Here I was, some twenty years later, timidly walking up to the door and ringing the bell. I had no idea what lay on the other side. The door slowly creaked open, revealing a gentle woman gracious enough to let me in and leave me to explore the house alone. While I was still filled with a sense of impending doom, I felt strangely empowered trudging down the steps to my teenage bedroom. I crept round the corner, gently offering a healing touch to the sheetrock that had been repaired from the many holes I punched in the walls.

Back when I lived there, I was such an angry kid. Of course, anger is always a secondary emotion; the unnoticed and unspoken hurt and rejection came long before my violent outbursts. I so badly wanted for someone to reach out and save me from myself and the mix of painful emotions I lived in.

No one ever came. I never gave anyone a chance.

I couldn't stand to let anyone get close to me. I verbally berated my closest friends and cheated on my girlfriends. I lied and stole from everyone. Self-protection ruled my life.

I had a special hatred for Christians. In tenth grade the girl with the locker next to mine once tried to share her faith with me. My only reply was to utter the name Satan in the creepiest voice I could manage. It disturbed her so much that I couldn't resist greeting her each day with the name, sometimes in a slow whisper, other times a loud shrill.

It was John Michael Talbot, the guitar-playing monk, and his slow songs set to biblical passages that began my change. I had borrowed my mom's car and was waiting for my friend to come back from our dealer's house. Suddenly I saw him sprint toward the car with two handfuls of pot.

"I went to take a piss and their bathtub was full of it! Quick! I need somewhere to hide it!"

I scurried around the vehicle looking for some container, and there before me written in black marker were the words "Hiding Place" on the spine of a cassette tape. I quickly filled the case and crammed the rest in an old bag of chips.

I was so humored by the fortuitous event that day that I decided to give the tape a listen. What flowed out of my old, spray-painted, candle-wax-covered stereo was a peace and safety I had never known. The bearded monk sang, "You are my hiding place, O Lord. You save me in my distress. You surround my soul with cries of deliverance."[6] Night after night I listened, stoned and curled up in a thick blanket, hiding from the darkness. Ever so gently my terror would subside as I drifted off to sleep.

I stole other John Michael Talbot tapes and hid them in my vast collection of hard-core punk rock and gangster rap.

I was such a hypocrite; I would curse Christians by day and each night cling to their God, begging for protection. I was the prodigal son who had burned his one chance and wasn't welcome back. I so longed for God yet hated the religion that had rejected and forgotten me.

I sort of fell apart the last couple of years I lived there. I was always high, smoking pot six or seven times a day. I hid from most of my friends, seldom bathed, and failed nearly all my classes. I thought I was crazy or possessed or both. I never could have imagined I would turn out to be the person I am today, but that is for another story.

Into my old bedroom I softly crept. I climbed on a chair, peering above the ceiling tiles just to make sure I hadn't left any pipes or porn behind. Pacing the room, I whispered my confessions—I named it all. I prayed that God's love and peace would fill every crack and crevice.

That day I exchanged my guilt for understanding. I had long since taken responsibility for my actions, but that day I was able to move beyond and see the big picture of who I was.

I felt a sort of pity for the broken and scared little boy I once had been. I'd been coping. I'd been surviving with the tools I had. Strangely, I found myself smiling at how much power and shame I had given to those years. Living in regret is a colossal waste of energy.

I left that house on Falkner Avenue with a big smile, a handful of homemade cookies, two jars of fresh jam, and a warm hug from the lady who now lives in my old home. More surprisingly, I left with a peace I never imagined possible. I felt empowered. I felt brave. I was free.

Over the next few days, as I emerged from my dark mining shaft of shame and secrets, I noticed a different tapestry in the Kansas landscape. It was early spring, and amidst the wind-torn, barren landscape, small green foliage was tenderly sprouting between dusty dead grass and prickly twigs. Forged in the cruelty of winter, the vegetation was strong and hardy yet gentle, a paradox of beauty.

I don't hate Kansas anymore. I'm saddened by what Kansas meant, what had happened, and who I was.

Colorado Once Again

It had been nine months since my redemption tour began, and I was back in Colorado to hang out with my dad for his birthday. After deciding to do some hiking in northern Colorado, it occurred to me that I could visit my college alma mater and the house my wife and I lived in when we were first married. Unbeknownst to my dad, he would serve as my confessional priest this time.

Each confession was easier; I was getting used to this. Again I felt free and released. But this time something different occurred. As I was recounting to my dad why I had done so poorly in college, I was left with the realization that it was rare for a professor not only to have gotten a GED but also to have spent time at a community college, a small Christian liberal arts school, and a small and a large state school. I knew well the strengths and weaknesses of each educational experience, and it greatly informed my teaching. My failures had given me a knowledge few possessed. That afternoon as we hiked, I began to name all the wonderful things that had come out of my life's negative choices. Goodness from darkness. Redemption.

I've never understood how people can say they don't have regrets in life. I can't imagine not wanting to change one single thing. Just because good has come out of bad doesn't mean we made the right choices. Is there even a need for forgiveness if we wouldn't change our choices? I live with a mess of regrets. Yet there is freedom and beauty in accepting who we are and who we have become. Good, bad, striving, victory, sin, heartache, joy, love, good times, boredom, success, failure, hurt feelings, the mundane, and excitement have all shaped who I am today. And I like myself. I think I can hold together the ideas that I wish I had made better choices and that my choices have also created who I am today.

What I learned that day and since is to appreciate the mistakes and circumstances in my life. In all honesty, I really have no clue what's good for me. But I do trust that God can work good out of the bad.

California

My dad was traveling with me again on this trip, and I asked if we could carve out a day to visit where I was born and the house we lived in. I didn't have anything to confess since I was under a year old when we moved, but I had never been back to the town I was born in and thought it might be good to see.

Traversing the giant Southern California boulevards, we visited all the sites of my father's upbringing. I listened as he lit up with story after story. He painted Norman Rockwell images of a little boy delivering newspapers in the morning hours. I tried hard to imagine that this crowded, dirty, noisy world was once a picturesque orange grove that my father skipped through on his way to school.

After two hours of gridlock traffic, we made it a few miles down the road to the hospital where I was born. After some research and a call to my mother, it was determined that I wasn't born in Canoga Park, as I had always been told, but rather in Woodland Hills. It was a little adjustment to realize I had been lying about my birthplace all these years, but it provided much humor for the rest of the day.

We walked through the neighborhood I lived in as an infant, a simple, nice place where the roses my mother planted some thirty-eight years ago still bloomed. It made me sad to think of the enthusiasm my parents must have felt when they started their family. I'm sure the growing-up years of my brother and me were not what they had expected. We make our plans, we hope and we dream—and then life happens.

As we once again sat for a couple of hours in traffic to travel a mere fifteen miles, I began to realize that lining my father's reflections were his own subtle confessions. He told about his first memory of doing something wrong—stealing an orange from the neighborhood farm—and about how he worked too much and wasn't attentive to his new wife.

What is it about visiting old memories that opens us up to confession? I wonder if confession is not just about naming our wrongdoings but is a deliberate act of framing our life in an honest and open manner, accepting the truth of our life and not trying to cover things up. Maybe confession doesn't just have to be a big thing we gear ourselves up for but can be a posture and a practice of living an open life with integrity and genuineness.

It now seems so simple: when we face our actions, resentments, and fears, the pain lessens. Keeping our secrets unspoken and bottled away is a guarantee of maintaining their power and destruction over us.

Most everyone believes the guilty should be punished. What does this mean if I harbor blame against myself? If I live with constant guilt and shame, how does this affect me? Do I end up punishing myself, if even on a subconscious level?

Confession brings a new acceptance of myself. I rest in my own skin, content. Only through confession am I able to see myself as God sees me: broken, hopeful, whole. I'm okay. I *am* okay. Confession is the road to self-acceptance and self-love. People who scoff at the notion of self-love either have never known the pain of self-hatred or have and don't believe any other way is possible. Confession is frightening and takes a courage far beyond what we traditionally define as strength. What I defined as strength growing up wasn't strength; that was pride and revenge.

The world is beautiful. The sun does shine. As surely as the rain comes, the plants grow. And the splendor of God runs rampant. Confession frees us to focus on things true, noble, right, pure, lovely, and admirable.[7]

Once again, the results far exceeded my efforts.

Confession
Frederick Buechner (1926–)

Carl Frederick Buechner was born in New York City in 1926. He is an ordained minister in the Presbyterian Church and has authored more than thirty books.

When Buechner was a young boy, his father committed suicide. This, no doubt, had a great impact on his literary work throughout the rest of his life. He completed his undergraduate studies at Princeton and served in World War II. Buechner's first novel, *A Long Day's Dying*, was met with success, and he intended to begin a literary career. It was around this time that Buechner was confronted with the words in a sermon by George Buttrick describing Jesus as being crowned "among confession, and tears, and great laughter." Buechner cites this moment as being the beginning of his transformation in Christ, which led him to pursue a seminary education at Union Theological Seminary, studying under such theological heavyweights as Paul Tillich and Reinhold Niebuhr. After seminary, Buechner continued to write while fulfilling ministerial appointments. But by 1967, he moved to Vermont to "give myself . . . more to the ministry of writing."

Buechner's writings are not explicitly Christian and would not necessarily fit in the genre of "Christian fiction." While some Christians confronted him for the content of his stories and his unwillingness to be more overtly Christian in his writings, many praised him for the honesty of his work. Buechner tells the truth within and through flawed characters and the frailty of the human condition. This commitment to being intellectually honest in his writing has allowed Buechner to maintain a wide readership of Christians and non-Christians alike.

Of confession he wrote, "I not only have my secrets, I am my secrets. And you are yours. Our secrets are human secrets, and our trusting each other enough to share them with each other has much to do with the secret of what it means to be human."

Many questioned his decision to attend seminary and possibly waste a literary career by going into the ministry, but the decision to follow this call led him to pave the way for American Christian confessional literature by such authors as Anne Lamott, Brennan Manning, and Henri Nouwen.

Understanding
Simplicity

Simplicity is an *inward* reality that results in an *outward* lifestyle. Both are necessary.

The inward reality of simplicity is beautifully encapsulated in Matthew chapter 6, especially Jesus's concluding words that we are to "seek first the kingdom of God" and the righteousness of this kingdom, and all that is needed for life will be added to us.[1] This laser-beam focus on a "with-God life" in God's kingdom *is* the inward reality of simplicity. As Jesus reminds us, when our eye is single, our whole body will be full of light.

Three key attitudes of heart help to summarize this internal focus. If what we have we can receive as a gift from God; and if what we have we know is to be cared for by God; and if what we have can be available to others when it is clearly right and good, then we are living in the inward reality of simplicity. But if what we have we feel that we alone have gotten; and if what we have we believe is up to us to hold on to; and if what we have we cannot make available to others when it is clearly right and good, then we are living in duplicity.

To experience the liberating interior spirit of simplicity *will* affect how we live, sometimes quite dramatically. However, we quickly learn that the outward lifestyle of simplicity will be as varied as individuals and the multifaceted circumstances that make up their lives. We must never allow simplicity to deteriorate into another set of soul-killing legalisms.

Nevertheless, it is possible to think in terms of certain controlling principles that can guide our decisions in the outward lifestyle of simplicity. For example, we can think in terms of buying things for their usefulness rather than their status. Or we can learn to reject anything that is producing an addiction in us. Or we can learn to enjoy many things without needing to own them. And we can develop many other similar principles. When our internal focus is clear, the Spirit of God will most certainly guide our outward decisions.

Always remember that simplicity is both a discipline and a grace. It is a discipline because we are called to do something. Simplicity does not just fall on our heads. We are to take up a consciously chosen course of action that involves both group and individual life. It is also a grace: a grace because the *life* that comes from our efforts is given to us by God. We know this by experience, for the results are always far in excess of the effort we put in. The life which simplicity brings is a supernatural gift to be graciously received.

In the midst of the Nazi terror, Dietrich Bonhoeffer said, "To be simple is to fix one's eye solely on the simple truth of God at a time when all concepts are being confused, distorted, and turned upside-down."[2] Such a focus will set us free from double-mindedness and enable us to cut through the Gordian knots of life.

Richard J. Foster

7

Simplicity

The Gift of Boredom

I have discovered that all the unhappiness of men arises
from one single fact, that they cannot stay quietly in
their own chamber.

Blaise Pascal[1]

Last year, I took a group of college students for two nights of
camping in the dense forest of northern Michigan as part of a
freshman orientation class I was teaching. Being present with
each other and God was the focus. I had only one rule: no phones.

It was a solid group, and in spite of sleeping under a tarp in
the rain, tipped canoes in icy water, and the slaughtering of a
chicken for dinner, everyone kept a positive attitude and was
quick to help out. Minus the dirty underwear someone put into
my sleeping bag, I felt respected as a leader. Yet, as it turned
out, many of my students individually snuck away with their
phones to text and post status updates.

I was mad. How could they neglect my simple rule? The next
week I prepared a guilt-inducing speech on their addiction to
technology and how they care more about shallow things than

about God. Then it hit me: I had used my phone too! Of course, it was justified; I needed a phone in case of an emergency. And when I began to miss my family, I determined it was good parenting to check in on the kids. Since I had my phone out, I might as well peek at my email; a quick reply might be needed. But I had no excuse for playing a game or checking eBay.

Isn't projection the force that propels us to spew self-righteous venom all over society? When I don't like something about myself, I feel a strange compulsion to teach others what they need to change; hypocrisy is a soothing salve for my festering shame.

I decided to let my speech go.

I'm romantically drawn to a simpler life. When I see an Amish carriage putter down the street, I feel nostalgic longing and jealousy churning. I'm quick to denounce their lifestyle as the result of faulty biblical interpretation and thus an unnecessary way to live. My weapon of cognition pacifies the fear that I lack their fortitude, and my desires to follow are left sedated.

The truth is that I want an oceanside castle complete with adjoining forest, lap pool, tennis court, skate park, theater room, and fancy garden with lots of fountains and birds. I would like to fly to France for coffee, shop without ever looking at a price tag, and be given box seats at Sundance and NBA games.

Yet, paradoxically, I'm infatuated with the monastic life of a ten-by-ten mountain cabin and days spent planting apple trees, talking to animals, and eating soup. I dream of being a mystic who regularly fasts forty days with ease and is content to live without the entertainment and extravagance of the Western world that I feel so entitled to. Simplicity requires sacrifices I'm not usually willing to make.

Throughout this process, I'm quickly learning that having a handful of experiences with each discipline is really just a beginning. The disciplines go deep, very deep, and deserve a lifetime of practice.

The discipline of simplicity is no different. In some ways it feels more difficult than the other disciplines because it goes so against the values of modern culture. It's hard to rip ourselves from this world where we are so ingrained with living hurried, unintentional lives filled with possessions and distraction.

My dad points out the importance of simplicity being an inward reality that results in an outward lifestyle. If it doesn't start inside, then my outward changes, even radical counter-cultural changes, are potentially superficial, leading to deadly legalism and never pushing me to deal seriously with the root problems of a consumer society. Simplicity is not necessarily about depriving ourselves of worldly things but about being content—content to have or do without, free to give but also receive.[2] It's about living free from the trappings of society that keep us from following Jesus's counsel to "seek first the kingdom of God."[3]

Seeking the kingdom involves a closer look at, and potential rejection of, our society's view of consumerism, materialism, wealth, accumulation, and the clutter of our lives. Kingdom living means I'm free to receive this world and free to give it up. We can only genuinely enjoy possessions without them destroying us when we are free to let them go and free to receive them.

The discipline of simplicity is to live from, as the Quaker writer Thomas Kelly refers to it, the "divine center."[4] Few things keep me from living in the divine center like my phone and the constant distractions it so often brings. Technology may be my greatest threat to living from the divine center. It's certainly the most consistent and socially acceptable threat.

Admittedly, I have much to learn about what it means to seek God's kingdom, but I'm pretty sure the way I use technology is mainly focused on building *my* kingdom. Whether I'm reading things to numb out, researching junk to buy, or looking for that ever-elusive social hit to remind me that I have some significance in the world, technology clutters my life. And oh, how I love it.

Yet I did wonder: What would it be like to spend a week without my phone, computer, and TV?

Sometimes it's best to just jump in, and so with Puritanical drama, curiosity overtook me and my unplugged week began. After triple-checking the automatic email bounces, I spent a good two hours obsessing over informing everyone who could possibly have any interest in contacting me that I would be unavailable. I walked away from my computer multiple times, only to race back on the verge of panic. What if someone thought I was deliberately blowing them off? I finally shouted to myself, "Leave it alone!"

Anxiously I walked around the block, trying to process what had just occurred. It wasn't like me to be overly concerned with pleasing others, but this stupid experiment had struck a frightful nerve. Why do I work diligently to be responsible and reliable? I guess I just don't want to let others down. But why? The answer seemed so simple, so silly: if I let people down, they may not like me and I might feel rejected, which would reinforce the lies I secretly believed about myself, and then I'd be forced to face the reality that your opinion of me matters and that I'm prone to let you define me. Oh crap! It was all about fear, and irrational fear at that.

The subtle pressure to be constantly available to others was a burden I had no idea I was carrying. I dropped it somewhere on the sidewalk that day. Sometimes we have to first let go of things in order to see them for what they are. My dependency on technology had been blinding me to the brokenness it was covering.

That evening I was out of sync. I kept feeling like there was something I was forgetting to do. Boredom crept in. I read a book and went to bed early.

Over the first few days, monotony seemed to be lurking in the cracks, especially at night. While my past experiences had taught me not to fear boredom and even to look for it as a friend and potential gift, I still missed the electric hit of affirmation from an email or message reminding me that I wasn't alone. The gentle fog of sadness settled in. When it came, I didn't run. I sat quietly in the divine center. I was simply being before God. It felt a lot like prayer, meditation, or solitude, and it was glorious.

Yet sometimes the sadness remained. This exercise was not easy; the desire to hide, cover, distract was a battle waging in my scattered self. If I waited long enough, I always felt rested, relaxed, and grounded. Waiting empowered me to face life and the emptiness that seems to be part of the universal human experience. I found I didn't have to fear the sadness. I was not alone. I was learning to be. And as the fourteenth-century mystic Julian of Norwich would say, "All shall be well, and all shall be well, and all manner of thing shall be well."[5] Through the discipline of simplicity, I was learning to sit quietly in my room. Pascal would be proud.

As the week wore on, I finished reading two books and had a new calm about me. Free from my digital tether, I began to explore the gift of boredom. I had been choking out stillness. Shooting off a handful of emails as I waited in the grocery store line or obsessively responding to texts throughout my day effectively cut out space for people, new thoughts and ideas.

As helpful as this experience had been, I was still overjoyed when the week came to an end and I was able to sift through the 102 messages that awaited me. Ironically, not a single one was of any importance. The world didn't miss me. A new question had found me: Just what is the cost of worshiping in the temple of efficiency and entertainment?

I left this experience determined not to go back to being a slave to my devices.

Through the years I've been greatly influenced by Dallas Willard's modern classic *The Divine Conspiracy*, where he draws attention to Jesus's notion that the kingdom of God is not just something in the afterlife but a here and now reality for us today.[6] Just how to live each day attuned to God's love and grace remains a mystery, but as I'm learning from this project, it seems to have a lot to do with simply being still, listening, and living in God's presence. Something happens when I tune my heart toward the gentle, mysterious tone of God's kingdom that seems to reverberate through all creation. Just as God seems to be found in quiet stillness, the essence of his presence seems to turn up in the simple. Simple, quiet, and ordered.

As my dad points out, I was on the journey to understanding that inward changes produce outward expression. You can't have one without the other. An inner transformed life always leads to outward expression, just as an outward expression void of inner change is nothing more than, as Jesus pointed out to the Pharisees, "whitewashed tombs."[7]

The disciplines were starting to make sense. They inherently form us to respond to life in a good and healthy way. When moral leaders have affairs, steal money, or get caught with porn, it's not a moment of moral lapse; it is only symptomatic of what's really going on behind what others see. It reveals their years of inner training in selfishness.

While our actions have natural consequences, the inner condition of our heart is not something to shame ourselves over; it's only an indication of our need to work on cultivating good spiritual habits. We don't need to fake or pretend. We are who we are: a people in process. And so, empowered by God's total acceptance of us, we become people learning to walk humbly through life, growing in our ability to respond to life in helpful ways. When we're living like Jesus—gentle, gracious, and strong—the fruit of the spirit quits being something we try for and becomes a natural outgrowth of our lives.[8]

This inner life may be reflected nowhere better than in how we treat others. According to Ignatius, if caring for the poor and oppressed and the hungry does not mark our church, then we are guilty of heresy. The outward expressions of the discipline of simplicity incorporate how we engage the world in relation to wealth, possessions, and materialism. And blatant disregard for the poor and disenfranchised only reveals our heart.

We are so embedded in a culture whose desire for wealth is borderline psychotic. We are a nation obsessed with protecting and expanding our individual rights and liberties. I can only imagine what good would come if we were as dedicated and fervent about fighting for the rights and liberties of those on the margins.

Whether we like it or not, our economic system's existence is dependent upon materialism. The low cost of goods we enjoy is only made possible by the exploitation of others. It's been a painful awakening to learn about just how much I benefit from the enslaved and impoverished labor force that produces virtually everything I buy. One of the positive aspects of an increasingly global society is the rise in awareness of the plight of the rest of the world. There are a myriad of issues involved in social problems with no easy answers, but I am encouraged to see a growing global consciousness. Many are now talking and writing about the atrocities of slave labor used to produce coffee, chocolate, diamonds, and other goods. The issue of sex trafficking is now a topic for Sunday sermons. It requires bravery to face the reality that we play a role in these evils. And even though we can feel so helpless and overwhelmed by the sheer gravity of these issues, I'm reminded it's not an excuse to do nothing, even if my efforts are meager.

In trying to deal with the inner condition that drives my consumerism, I decided to work on another fast related to simplicity by avoiding both shopping and advertising as best I could for a week. After making arrangements and a couple of rules related to food and going out with friends, I began.

The first thing I realized is just how subjected I am to marketing and advertising. It's absolutely everywhere. I consume it often without my own awareness. Wherever I turn, someone is trying to manipulate me into buying something. I interact with advertisements more than just about anything else. Reading the brands on clothes, cups, and signs is virtually impossible to avoid.

The second thing I noticed is that not only am I a good student of knowing various products and brands, but I like it—a lot. I get a small rush from knowing about new products. Dreaming and planning what I want to buy is almost a hobby of mine. I bid on eBay like a gambler. I search for deals, read product reviews, visit garage sales and gift shops, all the while the space in my house for holding all the stuff I buy is feeling smaller and smaller. The reality of my consumption of goods reveals my inner brokenness. It's a deep problem. I use consumerism as a drug—something to look forward to, to cheer me up, to excite me.

The divine center calls me to respond to the needs of others. God's love leads me to love others. When I hold on to possessions that I'm not using or enjoying, I'm depriving others from benefiting from them. And so, out of a desire to pursue simplicity even further and better align my actions with my beliefs, I took a couple more small steps and joined Amnesty International, sponsored another child, and vowed to buy used and fair trade items when available.

O God, help form me.

O God, help form us.

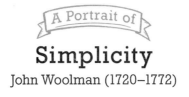

Simplicity
John Woolman (1720–1772)

Born to a Quaker family in New Jersey, John Woolman was one of the first anti-slavery voices in the Americas. His activism and writing for the abolition of slavery were influential to the abolitionist movement in both the American colonies and England.

At age eighteen, John left the family farm to work to become a prosperous shopkeeper. Woolman tried to sell practical items and not profit off others by selling on credit (a common business practice of the day). He was successful in running his own business, but he found his business to be "too cumbersome" and thought it conflicted with the Quaker desire "to be content with a plain way of living." Woolman sold his business to work as a tailor and tend to his apple orchard. These vocations were less demanding on his time and allowed him to travel as an itinerant minister.

Woolman believed plain, simple living to be of great benefit not only to the individual but also to society as a whole. He worked to formally condemn slaveholding in the Quaker communities. While all Quakers embrace pacifism, Woolman spoke out and wrote against the French and Indian War, even advocating that Quakers should refuse to pay taxes that were subsidizing the war. Woolman opposed the unjust treatment of Native Americans in the colonies. Recognizing that certain products were made primarily by slaves, Woolman refused to consume sugar, rum, and molasses to avoid perpetuating the slave trade. Because garment workers were often poisoned while dying fabrics, he even wore undyed clothes.

Understanding
Service

Service as a Christian spiritual discipline is difficult to capture in words. We learn about service best by watching it in action over an extended period of time.

When we see someone intently listening to another human being, we are witnessing service in action. When we see a person holding the sorrows of another in tender, loving care, we are witnessing service in action. When we see someone actively guarding the reputation of others, we are witnessing service in action. When we see simple, everyday acts of kindness, we are witnessing service in action. It is in these actions and many more like them that we begin to get a picture of service.

These tiny corners of life are the genuinely significant realities in the kingdom of God. There is no flash, no glitz, no titanic anything. Today's celebrity culture, captive to its pretentious egoism, simply finds such realities hard to grasp.

The towel and the basin are the icons of service. I am, of course, referring to the well-known story in John 13 where Jesus washed the feet of his disciples. In doing this he redefined for them—and for us—the meaning of greatness. After Jesus's startling act, he says, "Do you know what I have done to you? You call me Teacher and Lord—and you are right, for that is what I am. So if I, your Lord and Teacher, have washed your feet, you also ought to wash one another's feet. For I have set you an example, that you also should do as I have done to you."[1]

Now, the specific act of washing feet has genuine punch because it was simply a continuation of the whole of Jesus's life. From the hidden years in Nazareth to the self-sacrificing love of Calvary, all that Jesus was and did was a seamless robe of service. Do you remember that it was said of Messiah that he would not "break a bruised reed or quench a smoldering wick"?[2] Jesus, you see, would never crush the needy; he would never snuff out the smallest hope. This is service in action.

Of all the spiritual disciplines, service is the most conducive to the growth of the grace of humility within us. This is good news indeed, for we all know that humility is not one of those things that comes to us by trying to get humility. No, we must come at this most prized virtue through the indirect route of routine acts of service.

William Law, in his classic work *A Serious Call to a Devout and Holy Life*, urges us to make every day a day of humility. And how are we to do this? Law counsels, "Condescend to all the weaknesses and infirmities of your fellow creatures, cover their frailties, love their excellencies, encourage their virtues, relieve their wants, rejoice in their prosperities, compassionate their distress, receive their friendship, overlook their unkindness, forgive their malice, be a servant of servants, and condescend to do the lowest offices to the lowest of mankind."[3] You see, it is through simple, daily acts of service that the grace of humility will slip in on us unawares.

The risen Christ beckons us to the ministry of service. Such a ministry, flowing out of the inner recesses of the heart, is life and joy and peace.

Richard J. Foster

Service

Can I Be Your Martyr?

> The flesh whines against service but screams against
> hidden service. . . . Every time we crucify the flesh, we
> crucify our pride and arrogance.
>
> Richard J. Foster[1]

A few years ago, in a moment of desperation and vulnerability,
I poured out a lengthy narrative to a friend about how my life
was falling apart.

"Nate, time for you to go serve," he callously responded.

"No, you don't understand. Things are falling apart!"

"Oh, I do understand. It's time for you to pull your head out
of your a** and go serve. Take out the trash, mow your neighbor's yard, and I bet your wife could use a break from the kids."

As my mom once told me, "The truth will set you free . . .
usually right after it pisses you off!" This was to be the case.

It took months for me to realize the treasure my friend had
given me. The haze of selfishness so often clouds my ability to
see life's problems as they really are. Service may be the most
effective tool at revealing the parameters of just how encompass-
ing my self-centeredness is.

On paper I look like a guy who knows a lot about service. For ten years I worked as a social worker in a variety of settings, pouring my professional energies into people who had been abused, marginalized, sick, and poor. For the last eight years, while teaching college students how to care for the needy in our society, I've managed to devote time to developing significant mentoring relationships with a number of them. I have a stack of thank-you cards and letters to prove just how refined I've become at practicing the discipline of service. Yet my years of practice are misleading, because my motives remain a mess of selfish desires. I serve for a number of reasons, often having little to do with trying to be truly helpful to others. Not only does service work feed my need for worth and value, but being engaged in the details of the lives of others helps me feel better about my own problems. Working with others provides a safe, one-sided intimacy.

If we're to be true to the words and life of Jesus, then the first criteria for leadership should be a life of genuine and sincere service. We shouldn't ask who has charisma and flash but who among us are the greatest servants. It only takes a couple of confident voices in leadership calling us to follow the Jesus life to cure our religious communities of our obsession with bigger, better, slicker, noisier kingdoms erected in our own honor.

How I wish this were the example I saw around me as a young man. Now, in many contexts, it is my turn to lead—as a professor, as a speaker and writer, as a father, as a man—and I fear I lack the courage and strength that years of studying the example of others would have given. Oh, how I long for more models of the countercultural servitude that Jesus provided to challenge and shape me.

Selfishness is the universal human shortcoming that fuels every evil. Those who lack awareness of their malady may just be the sickest of us all.

Jesus so beautifully deals with the disciples' desires to be recognized as great, telling them, "If you want to be first, be last. Be the biggest servant."[2] And then he so humbly, so scandalously gets on his knees and washes their mud-caked feet. The best form of teaching: example. As my dad says, "True service rests content in hiddenness. It does not fear the lights and blare of attention, but it does not seek them either. Since it is living out of a new Center of reference, the divine nod of approval is completely sufficient."[3]

I so deeply want the divine nod of approval to be enough. So for this project I went looking for service that doesn't bring attention. In keeping with the theme of the verse I memorized earlier, I went looking for ordinary, simple, everyday ways of practicing the discipline of service.

The unemployment rate in my town is one of the highest in the nation. Adults regularly knock on my door looking for odd jobs. It occurred to me that paying them to do work not only helps me out, but is a small way I can serve. It's an opportunity to bring dignity and respect.

The neighborhood kids constantly want to come over. They are loud and needy and always make a mess. To practice service, I quit begrudgingly letting them over and later complaining about it and instead decided to welcome their presence as a little death of myself. I opened up my house, and in a small way my heart, to them. It became an opportunity to serve kids who seemed to get very little male attention. Good things came out of our times together. I became more patient, less controlling, and more intentional.

Ever notice how much of our behavior is just following the norms and practices we've been taught without ever really looking at their purpose or even their value? For example, when parking a car, we look for the best space, even if that means driving up and down the aisles. We get in the shortest checkout line and scurry to take the last piece of dessert at the cafeteria.

In traffic we move into the lane moving the fastest. We do all these things instinctively to get ahead. Is our time really more valuable than that of others? Is this how we love our neighbor? How does the Jesus way of choosing to be last play out in our lives? We lobby for our rights and pay at work—when do we fight for others? Do we even think about others at all?

My experience with service had begun a small shift in the way I look at life. For eight years I've been a professor at a small liberal arts university. Each spring when the university crowns a professor with the teacher of the year award, I'm always taken with an uncomfortable mix of emotions: I'm excited, nervous, hopeful, and then disappointed and jealous. I really wish I didn't want to win the award, but I do. Recently I started doing something different. I started praying I wouldn't win. Instead I prayed that a colleague of mine who really needed the encouragement and affirmation would win the award. And as I sat in the chapel and listened to the beautiful announcement of that year's recipient, I cried for joy at her accomplishment. Rather than feeling the usual disappointment and jealousy, I was happy, content, and maybe even joyful.

In the following months I passed by all the good parking spaces, I took the worst seat in a meeting, I stood last in a line, I left the last piece of cake at the cafeteria, and I let others board the plane before me. In every situation, I sought to become last. All of these acts became little deaths of my desire to be first, to have my own way, and it felt good. While these actions may seem like simply being overly polite, something deep was working within me. Not only were these small ways to practice neighbor love, but each gesture seemed to move me into a more conscious awareness of each moment and my response to life. The normal hurry and anxiety of my days were strangely dissipating. It's hard to be frantic when you're purposely looking to serve others.

"Hurry is greed," my friend Robert casually muttered one day. "You're just trying to escape your own mortality. You have limited energy and time—accept it." This got me thinking about the manner in which I spend my time. Is it greed when I'm trying to be super productive? Am I not accepting my human limitations and trying to take more than my share? Certainly by our standards Jesus was really unproductive. He spent thirty years in a broken-down, working-class town doing what? In his ministry he really only invested in twelve guys, and even they didn't seem to understand what he was really trying to do. He didn't write books or leave clear, concise discipleship methods. Jesus even gave the responsibility of furthering his message to Peter, the guy who had just ditched him. According to worldly values, his service work was inefficient. Jesus was relaxed; we are stressed. Jesus was patient; we are obsessed with progress. Jesus was content; we want more. Jesus's church was small; we insist on mega.

Greed is disruptive. Greed makes me miserable. It shuts me in and closes me off from God. Giving opens me up so God can come in. Here comes that joy thing again. Letting someone go ahead of me in a checkout line results in joy? Weird.

As with the other disciplines, after a week or two of being intentional with the practice, it had already become a sort of habit. I don't really have to think much about my actions now; my instinct is to let others go first. Sure, sometimes I still take the last slice of pie or rush to the front of the line, but now it's different. I smile at God and we talk about what I'm doing and the silliness of me wanting to have my own way. You don't have to be perfect to live in the divine nod of approval; you just have to show up. He already accepts us. His love is everywhere; I just choose to connect to it.

Recently I revealed to a group of men that I wanted my tombstone to read, "He loved well," and that my life and career goals were now to follow suit and this primarily meant being a good husband and father.

"You're crazy! You can't set loving your family as the main goal of your life," one man stammered, shaking his head. "You'll fail—they know you too well. But it's brave; I'll give you that. It's brave."

His doubts only shored up my resolve. It's easy to win the admiration and approval of people who see only one side of you. Serving at home is complicated, because not only can it lack the accolades you might get elsewhere, but you just can't fake it at home. A good spouse calls out the true you, refusing to let you live in the false realities of who you might think you are. I have a good spouse . . . a really good spouse.

Something feels countercultural about choosing to abandon my career aspirations in order to love and serve my family. Men used to use bravery to hunt and fight. I use mine to do the dishes, wash poop off the dog, and carpool the kids. I am learning to not act like a martyr. Helping is a conscious choice.

During Christmas break I decided to take service to the next level, face my fears, and do something that would be a significant gift to my wife. While I disliked the old, moldy boxes from my childhood that I moved from house to house, they really bothered Christy. Taking care of them could be a huge gift to her.

Flashlight in hand, I peered into my shed and repeatedly tapped my foot to scare the mice away from the old, dilapidated stacks of boxes. My thoughts ran through all of the reasons I shouldn't sort through them, the kind of excuses that would come from a hoarder.

I lined up a couple of tasty snacks and blared my favorite cleaning album, U2's *War*. (Something about listening to the world of political unrest and the plight of others reminds me that not only is cleaning out things I have neglected or hoarded a first-world problem, but whether I keep or throw away my grade school field day ribbons is of extremely small significance compared with the day the majority of the people around the world are facing.) With the voice of Bono chanting in the background, I cleared a space in my cramped little garage, lined up thirty boxes I had brought in from the shed, held on to invisible courage, and jumped in.

I tried to make this a prayerful experience by inviting God into the process of sifting through the boxes and asking what to throw away, what to keep, give, file, or read, and what to remember. As with so many things in life, the project was about momentum. Once the inertia was broken, continuing wasn't hard at all. Within half a day I was really starting to enjoy the task. Confronting objects that symbolized sadness and regret was balanced with the happiness of unearthing a once cherished but long forgotten memory or treasure: psychotic poetry from my youth, failing-grade report cards, cute love notes from a grade school crush, first edition comic books, strange wooden carved figures from Costa Rica, and old Beatles records.

I spent the next two weeks working in the garage. Having to make decisions constantly was mentally trying, but I gave myself the freedom to not have to be perfect with what I kept or gave away. It really helped knowing that by giving items away, I would potentially be blessing someone. I kept telling myself that if in the next year I found I should have kept something, I could always replace it, even if I ended up spending a couple hundred dollars on old tools or clothes. Isn't it worth that amount to have an uncluttered life? My task was to work on clearing the clutter, and as I did, what once felt overwhelming and weighed me down was quietly replaced with a growing sense of empowerment. I was choosing to live in a much simpler way. Again, one discipline melded into the next—service into simplicity. And while I suspected my journey with simplicity was just beginning, I felt freer. That feeling I had reserved for Santa appeared once more: joy. Joy is exactly what I felt when I took ten boxes of old paper to recycling and four vanloads of stuff to Goodwill.

I was so enthusiastic about this service project that I decided to take on another around the house. My wife had been getting into cooking, and I thought it might be helpful to give our kitchen and laundry room a thorough cleaning and reorganizing. Over the next week I gutted the entire kitchen and scrubbed the cracks and crevices with a toothbrush. With manic enthusiasm, I jumped into this project, and it was fun. I was so excited to have a newly organized and labeled kitchen. Finishing sooner than planned, I next moved into organizing the living room and closets.

After devoting an entire week to giving my wife such a selfless gift, you can imagine my shock when in the following days she wasn't adhering to my tidy, labeled system. I, of course, expressed my confusion and frustration in a strong, dramatic tone.

It's usually not until a couple of hours after a fight that I'm able to make any rational sense of what was being said. Sometime later that night, my righteous anger at her ingratitude for all I had done was replaced with the stark realization that my little "service project" had a whole lot more to do with me and my desire for spotless order than with doing something she actually wanted done. I had misinterpreted her enthusiasm for what I was doing—she was just happy I was engaging in caring for our home and glad to see me take ownership of the kitchen. Altruistic service has no expectations or ties to the actions of those you are serving. True service does not create martyrs.

I went into this project aware of how sometimes I do service work for selfish reasons, yet it happened again. How easy it is to blind ourselves. I guess it makes sense to ask others what they need rather than assuming I know best. Unfortunately, this failure is the history of many of nations' and churches' mission aid work. By assuming we know what people need and seldom if ever asking, we end up disempowering those we're trying to serve.

Yet service by its very nature will make us less selfish people. It's not that we need to ignore our desire for attention or even hide from it when it comes. Rather, we should be free to give and receive. The true gift of service comes not from the praise of others but from the joy that results from a life content with coming in last and freedom from the trappings of greed. And even though selfish motives may be what propel us into a giving life, God can untangle even the messiest of knots if our hearts remain open to him. We discover the divine order of things: that when we give, we actually receive.

And if this is true, our failure to let others serve us is actually depriving them of growth, of a gift. Feeling like we have to be strong, like we can't let others serve us, is actually selfish weakness. Jesus let people wash his feet and pour oil on him.[4] Jesus asked for help.

Service
Jane Addams (1860–1935)

Considered the pioneer of the field of social work, Addams was the daughter of a wealthy Illinois state senator. She chose to eschew marriage in favor of living a life of service among the poor and immigrant communities of Chicago.

Her mother passed away when Addams was a toddler. Educated at Rockford Female Seminary, she went on to study at Woman's Medical College of Pennsylvania, only to abandon her studies upon the death of her father. She then spent a few years traveling in Europe.

Addams believed that private charity was having little impact on the urban poor and set forth to give of herself. She moved into a poor, multiracial neighborhood in Chicago and went on to develop the Hull House settlement to serve the community. The Hull House was never overtly religious, but Addams's faith was central to the reasons she founded it.

Addams joined the women's suffrage movement in 1907. She believed that once women achieved the right to vote, other social reforms would follow more quickly. Outraged by the start of World War I, she tirelessly worked to advocate for peace during the war.

In 1931, a few years before her death, she was recognized for her lifetime of service to others as the first American female recipient of the Nobel Peace Prize.

What is unique about Addams's life of service is that she didn't just give money or serve from afar but was willing to radically alter her lifestyle to make service something she was, not just something she did.

Interlude

Discipline Hazard #2:
My Inner Pharisee

Walk cheerfully over the world, answering that of God
in everyone.

George Fox[1]

When I came back from practicing the discipline of solitude in
Virginia, the noise and chaos of home was in such contrast to
the solitude I had experienced that I couldn't handle the adjustment. At first it seemed that spending time in solitude made my
life harder, like how when you come back from visiting a warm
climate during the winter, at first you're freezing. It takes a while
to adjust. I have come to realize that I hadn't worked with solitude enough for its benefits to integrate into my everyday life.
I've since learned to carry pieces of the silence with me. Solitude
takes away the anxious edges of frantic bosses, hurried deadlines,
and sick kids, therefore allowing us to see the sacred in it all.

In the rolling hills and frigid woods of southwest Michigan
is an old restored barn, the centerpiece of a retreat center called
the Hermitage. It's a modest place, with hiking trails and meals
served in silence. I have spent a number of nights in that old
barn. She has become a safe place for me.

The first two times I went there, I was fearful of the emptiness
and the boredom that I knew the stillness would bring. That

dread soon passed. The silent meals were another matter. I felt uncomfortable; the silence was so claustrophobic that I almost got up and left. I started taking a book to the meals. I never actually read it, but knowing it was there brought me comfort. It wasn't until my third trip to the Hermitage that I began to understand and appreciate the beauty of the silent meals. How often we clutter our lives with words. I was reminded of a quote from J. Brent Bill: "Words that linger in our hearts are often more helpful than those that pass quickly through our brains"[2]—and out our mouths. I discovered how eating together in silence was a way to practice being with others and not having to fill the air with noise. It was a way to dwell in deep community. After three days of sharing meals together, I felt genuinely connected to people whom I had never spoken to. It was fun to wonder about their stories. What were my silent companions escaping from or going home to? As I very gently and softly took my bites, I would pray about the anxiety or joy that was in their faces. A couple of times, after the meal was done, some of us chose to remain seated, together lost in the sacredness of the moment while the Spirit brooded about.

Just as I became comfortable with eating in silence, along came Mr. Bluetooth. Who eats breakfast at a silent retreat center with a Bluetooth phone headset dangling from their ear? Not only had he taken my seat, but he sat there aggressively thumbing through a magazine, grunting and sighing at every page. And then the way he devoured his food, smacking and slurping, not only was disgusting, it was loud. Was he trying to make noise? The monkish stillness I was cultivating was entirely disrupted. Didn't he know this was a sacred place? What was he doing here anyway? Then the real issue occurred to me: it wasn't Bluetooth and his blatant disregard for the stillness that was the problem; it was me and my judgment.

Jesus's words rung out, "For in the same way you judge others, you will be judged."[3] I've found this verse helpful in thinking about how we judge ourselves. It's almost become a cliché that people who speak loudly against homosexuality end up involved in some gay scandal. Or how skinny people obsessed with their own weight are judgmental and cruel toward heavier people. Our judgments of others most likely say more about us and the condition of our hearts than they say about others. Pointing out the splinter in my brother's eye and ignoring the plank in my own[4] helps me minimize what I don't like about myself. My inner critic cannot be contained and spews over onto others. Legalism is a horrid bondage.

How quickly I had forgotten my experience with silent meals in Virginia, when I had been goofing around to cover my own anxiety. How quickly I moved from throwing food to piously throwing judgment. I wish I could say my judgment was an isolated incident, but it is not.

While my time with the disciplines has brought failures, in many ways I think it's going great. Yet despite all I've learned, I've noticed a subtle arrogance and a slight disparagement of others brewing. In my efforts to present my body as a living sacrifice, to intensively and intentionally do a series of these spiritual activities, I had started to eye the behavior of others. I had begun to swell with pride—the fruit of hell. Could this be a danger of practicing the spiritual disciplines? After all, the religious leaders of Jesus's day practiced disciplines with intensity and dedication that few have rivaled, yet despite their religious fervor, spiritual acts seemed little more than a tool used to control and oppress or impress others. Would they not have been better off being a real thief or prostitute, rather than a religious one?

I've known my share of well-intentioned, judgmental, legalistic, religious folks, and I'd rather be just about anyone besides one of them. Who does more life-crushing damage in our society, the sinners or the supposed saints? Jake is a dirty homeless man who panhandles by day and drinks himself to sleep by night. The guy ditched his family and his kids don't even know where to find him, but he's always eager to share what little he has, and with loving care he guides the newly homeless and watches after the sick. If you overdose, you can count on Jake to get you help. In his drunken stupor, he strums out worship tunes and prays for his community, begs God for forgiveness for his mistakes, and is known for his love. Then there are those who fool themselves into thinking they are helping others while hell-bent on shaming and controlling everyone, manipulating anyone within earshot, proof-texting the Bible as they dangle the keys to eternal life and, with gusto and charm, threaten damnation to those who don't follow their legalistic and judgmental path.

I don't want to be either one, but if I had to choose, I think I'd opt for living under a bridge and loving rather than trying to be God.

"Hey Dad, have you noticed how the disciplines can create legalism?"

"Nate, I don't get it." He sighed. "I've tried so hard to make it clear that the disciplines are not a system of blessedness. They don't give us one bit of righteousness, but for some reason people will use them as a spiritual to-do list or something to beat themselves up about."

"What do you think about the idea that if the spiritual life has not led us to grace and freedom, then we have missed the point?"

"Absolutely. It's about freedom, not bondage. The disciplines are simply a means to train our mind and body. They place us in a position to live with God. It's not about trying to make something happen."

Later my dad counseled me to be honest about my judgment, realizing that it wasn't a reason to stop doing an exercise but a reason to continue as a way to help my brokenness, to move me closer to humility and graciousness toward others. The exercises are probably not producing the judgment but rather revealing what's been in my heart all along.

It's the older brother in the prodigal son story all over again. The father is so eager to celebrate the return of his son, and the older brother refuses to even go in the house.[5] Envious. Jealous. Bitter. Through the years I've almost come to relate more to the older brother than to the prodigal. Clearly the prodigal doesn't understand the grace and love the father is so eager to pour upon him, but neither does the older brother. He thinks he's earned the father's approval. But his trouble goes much deeper. Because he has been successful, he thinks that approval and love were things he earned, and here we find him actively trying to keep the father from extending grace to his broken, wayward son. Now, of course, the younger brother is a self-centered mess who has no idea he's loved unconditionally, but the older brother is almost pathological. He reveals what happens when a person living out of the self-hatred narrative actually succeeds in their efforts. If my actions define who I am, then when I do really well, pride takes over and judgment settles in. I didn't need grace, so I'll actively try to keep it from you. I think it's that older brother mentality that Jesus was talking about when he told the Pharisees they turn their converts into twice the children of hell.[6]

This parable once again raises the question, "Who is closer to the kingdom?"

The disciplines reveal our shortcomings. I'm beginning to see that practicing the disciplines for any reason other than as a response to love is potentially dangerous. For if we feel like we fail at the disciplines, then they just become twelve new reasons to beat ourselves up. Or worse, if we think we have mastered them, we're on our way to becoming bitter and resentful, the hidden bondage of a smug and judgmental soul that only legalism can create.

Yet I'm not suggesting that if we do not know God's love, or find ourselves incapable of giving an active response to God's love, we should avoid the disciplines. Rather, we focus our efforts on activities that help reorient us to a truthful view of ourselves. We ask God to invade our minds with the truth about who we are, to inhabit our very cells. We pray and listen. We meditate on Bible passages related to our worth and identity. We let God draw us to spaces and activities that attend to our brokenness and disordered views. We confess our self-hatred. We submit to truth and not the beatings of shame. We refuse to practice hating something God so dearly loves. We learn to enter into a spiritual rest. We move in the rhythms of grace.

I really like how Jesus never had a harsh word for the broken but railed, with very colorful language, on those who thought they had it all together. I wonder if the harsh words were what they needed to crack their pompous shells. The sinners knew of their brokenness; the religious didn't. I'm starting to think pride is the biggest hindrance to the Christian life.

And so, as my judgment snuck its way in during breakfast with Mr. Bluetooth, I went back to the well of God's love and acceptance. Pride can't live in the face of my true identity. In the silence I listened. I confessed my pride. I prayerfully laughed at how easily I am seduced by self-righteousness. I wondered if I could even handle it if my outward behavior and the person I want to be inside actually lined up. Growth of all kinds comes with new challenges and opportunities.

For the Pharisee in me, it's an issue of identity, value, and my position as a much-loved child of God empowered by grace to show up for life, to be present to each moment, learning to live as Jesus would if he were to live my life.[7] I turn from the seduction of pride and the arrogance of judging others. But I also refuse to live in shame as the proverbial worm that's always striving but never measuring up. Grace says something different. Grace says we are sons and daughters of the Most High. Grace says we're loved and accepted just as we are. Right here. Right now. We should probably get this straight before attempting to love our neighbor as we love ourselves. The big brother did just that to his younger brother: he loved his brother as he loved himself. The stick he used to measure himself he extended to his brother. He offered the same love and grace he extended to himself every day—"Buck up and earn it!"

And yet grace and love do not mean that we don't set boundaries or make assessments of constructive and destructive behavior. Grace tells us the truth. Love oftentimes says no. This is much different than being a self-damaging victim-martyr or a self-promoting, scornful Pharisee. True grace changes us. Love enables freedom that allows us to accept ourselves exactly where we are so that we can become who the Father sees. Shame and condemnation do not help us respond to life as Jesus did. There is something very practical about the love and grace Jesus offers the broken; it works. Accepting God's unconditional love isn't feel-good self-help; it is central to the gospel. And through the years we will find it impossible to hate that which God loves. Frequently this begins with the way we treat and view ourselves. Nothing kills the self-hatred narrative that plagues modern culture more effectively than living in God's smile.

I'm also beginning to wonder if it is dangerous to approach the disciplines as a to-do list. If I'm able to regularly check them off, I might entirely miss the point of engaging in an intimate and honest relationship with a Father who accepts me without condition, thus opening the door to the judgmental, bitter smugness that only a life enslaved to legalism can construct. On the other end of the spectrum, if I don't feel like I measure up, I can begin to see God as just another press on my already taxed time, reminding me that I don't measure up. Then the guilt and shame take over and I'd just as soon avoid the disciplines altogether.

Practicing the disciplines out of an active response to God's love is a good place to start. However, I'm reminded that the practices are often what bring us to this posture. So we must begin with grace and acceptance.

I once met up with Father Terry, my friend and mentor from Kansas, while he was camping in the Colorado mountains. I entered his vintage popup tent, and there, lit by candlelight, was a print of Rembrandt's painting of the prodigal son.

"Nate, I've been working with this painting all week," Father Terry told me. "I've been the prodigal and I've been the older brother. These days I'm learning what it means to be like the father, to be a grace extender, to wait by the fence for people, to suffer over the brokenness of others."

I wonder if becoming like the father is the natural result of Christian spiritual formation.

I've been thinking about the big picture my dad mentioned at the beginning of this project and his discouragement that people don't seem to understand the disciplines as an all-encompassing divine means of grace for the transformation of the human personality. We enter into relationship with God as a response to grace. The disciplines enable us to become someone we were previously unable to be. That too is an act of grace. As Dallas Willard used to say, "The results from the disciplines far exceed what we put into them." This is how we become Christlike.

The clearest evidence of a person's spiritual formation is that they have become someone whose life is bathed in God's love, someone freely able to give and receive grace. Someone known for love.[8]

Understanding
Prayer

Prayer is the heart's true home. But, you see, we have been in a far country. It's been a country of climb and push and shove. It's been a country of noise and hurry and crowds.

The heart of God is an open wound of love because of this distance and preoccupation of ours. God mourns that we do not draw near to him. God weeps over our obsession with "muchness" and "manyness."

And God is seeking after us. God seeks us like the father rushing out to embrace the prodigal. God seeks us like the woman who will leave no stone unturned in her determination to find a lost coin. God seeks us like the shepherd searching, searching, searching for one lost sheep. God is seeking us.

God invites us to come home: home to where we belong; home to serenity and peace and joy; home to intimacy and acceptance and affirmation.

God welcomes us into the living room of his heart where we can put on old slippers and share freely. God welcomes us into the bedroom of his rest where we can be naked and vulnerable and free. It is also the place of deepest intimacy where we can know and be known to the fullest.

And it doesn't matter if we have little faith, or none. It doesn't matter if we have been bruised and broken by the pressures of life. It doesn't matter if our prayers have grown cold and brittle. It doesn't matter if God seems remote and inaccessible.

Just like a little child can never draw a bad picture, so a child of God can never utter a bad prayer. God, you see, accepts us just the way we are, and he accepts our prayers just the way they are.

But here is the beauty of this interactive life of prayer: God does not leave us the way we are. God's intention is to transform our inward character into the likeness of Christ. C. S. Lewis writes that God's intent for you and me is to form us into "a dazzling, radiant, immortal creature, pulsating all through with such energy and joy and wisdom and love as we cannot now imagine, a bright stainless mirror which reflects back to God perfectly (though, of course, on a smaller scale) His own boundless power and delight and goodness."[1] The interactive life of prayer is a central means God uses for bringing this transformative reality into the deep habit structures of our lives.

Now, we must not think of prayer as a flat, dull, one-dimensional experience. Far from it! Prayer is a dance, a love feast, a wrestling match, a high, hilarious party . . . I could continue adding metaphors for some time. Prayer is so rich and varied and individualized a reality.

The syntax of prayer is love. "True, whole prayer is nothing but love," writes Augustine of Hippo.[2] "The Trinity is our everlasting lover," declares Julian of Norwich.[3] "Jesus, lover of my soul, let me to Thy bosom fly," cries out Charles Wesley.[4]

The heart of God is open wide to receive us; we are welcome to come home.

Richard J. Foster

Prayer

Gifts from Bill

It is better in prayer to have a heart without words, than words without a heart.

Mahatma Gandhi[1]

Bill was a tall, larger-than-life figure who had the articulation, finesse, and rhythm characteristic of a 1950s preacher. My first memory of him was when he came to pray for me as a teenager. I'm not entirely sure what brought him to my room, but I do remember that those were the days of my misguided attempts to try to please God. I had worked hard at perfecting my legalistic view of faith and regularly practiced ruthless judgment toward others and myself. So you'll understand my shock when this Lutheran pastor laughed in the middle of his prayer. I don't think he understood that God required seriousness when being addressed. But my shock was brought to a whole new level and my respect for him plummeted when, with passion and intensity, he prayed the following words: "God, would you clean up all the s*** in Nate's head?"

My next significant encounter with Bill came years later after a midnight incident in which my substance abuse landed me in an ER, bloodied, getting a CAT scan and multiple stitches, which resulted in my wife asking me to not return home until I had gotten sober and sought help. Eventually, I made it to Bill's place, where he spent three days praying for me. As you might expect, I was filled with shame and embarrassment. I tucked my head in my lap as I recounted the previous months of my journey. I was amazed when Bill responded to my shame with laughter. When the astonishment of his reaction wore off, I began to see his message. His laughter was saying that everything was going to be all right; that while my life was out of control, things could be okay. This brought tears to my eyes. Though I didn't know it at the time, his countenance was exactly what I needed. In the proceeding days he treated me with such care and tenderness, fully believing that I could get sober and that life awaited me. While my last drink was still a few days away, this experience was a hinge in my healing process.

That was nearly twelve years ago. That time with Bill began a transformation not only in my life in general but in my prayer life as well. More important than teaching me to pray using honest and sincere language, Bill taught me about using my imagination when I pray. I had never really thought much about my imagination; it was simply a source of creative inspiration or fantasy.

In those days I viewed prayer as little more than an opportunity to recite a laundry list of desires and needs, occasionally sprinkling in a good confession and maybe a couple of praises from time to time. If asked, I would have told you it was relational and sometimes even intimate. But through the years, it's become something entirely different.

Now when I pray, I create movements in my mind. I push my attention toward a person or situation. I spend a lot of my prayer time simply sitting with God, thinking and listening while we exchange pictures of what we would like to see happen—co-creating. I was recently praying about an event where I would be speaking, and I imagined the Holy Spirit brooding about, filling the room, covering the cracks, and then I thought of the people, and I saw their frustration, their disillusionment with life and maybe even God. I turned my attention to the Father, and I felt his longing for them. I pray with hunches, movements, and nudges. It's a flow, a dance, a movement of grace bathed in love. I don't disconnect. I pray with my eyes open.

I'm sure I'll get at least a couple of emails from people eager to correct my ways as not biblical or to say that I'm really worshiping Hjarna, the Swedish Paleolithic God of the mind, and thus putting my soul in danger of eternal damnation. Please don't bother. While I try to remain teachable and open to the insights of others, I'm finding I have little interest in learning from extreme fundamentalists whose lives and careers are based on criticizing others—you know, those people who call themselves Christians but seem to know nothing of love.

Bill showed me that God can redeem and use this amazing tool he crafted within us—imagination—and that it should not be left out just because I am afraid of my own humanness. My fear had more to do with my lack of faith in God to guide and restore his own creation.

Another mentor of mine, in a sense, has been Brother Lawrence, the seventeenth-century Frenchman who wanted to serve the servants of God, so he went to wash dishes in a monastery. "The lord of all pots and pans," he was sometimes called. All we really know about him comes from a collection of his letters and journal entries about his experiments in attempting to take Paul's call to "pray without ceasing"[2] seriously by trying to stay in God's presence through as much of his day as possible. As with most new habits, it's best to start small and forsake our silly need for quick or perfect results. Failure only happens when we don't start. Humility can be an effect of not achieving our desired goals and may be a part of the learning process.

To practice the spiritual discipline of prayer, I decided to renew my own commitment to Brother Lawrence's idea of "practicing the presence of God."

Praying without ceasing is like calling a friend on the phone and never hanging up. I seek to maintain an ongoing conversation with God as I go about my day. It reminds me of spending the day with my wife or a close friend; we don't have to talk to be aware of each other's presence. I'm amazed at the way Christy and I can communicate without speaking, and it seems the same with prayer. I soon find it's a little like carrying with me what I find in solitude or worship—staying in a gentle posture, attuned to the movements of the Spirit as I go about my day. As the hours wear on, I often forget about God, and so I humbly begin again with grace and a smile at my limitations.

The analogy of athletic or musical training continues to apply. The more I practice, the stronger and more proficient I become. Again, prayer is not something to be mastered in forty days; forty years seems more applicable. Actually, it's not something to be mastered at all. As Thomas Merton said, "We do not want to be beginners [at prayer], but let us be convinced of the fact that we will never be anything but beginners, all our life."[3]

Muscle memory is the neurological process that happens with repeated activity, much like when someone learns to ride a bike or a baby learns to walk. The theory is that we lay new neural pathways each time we perform a certain movement. This is exactly how I felt when I started climbing mountains. It was almost as if the more mountains I climbed, the more my body knew how to do it. In a sense each mountain was easier, even if it had been a year since the last one and I wasn't in the physical shape I had been in before. Once I started to climb, my body seemed to remember how to endure the physical strain.

I wonder if this is how the spiritual life plays out as well. Throughout the years I have been practicing praying without ceasing, more so at some times than others, but as I began this project, it came back rather easily. Years ago, holding my attention on God for more than a few minutes seemed nearly impossible. These days it flows fairly smoothly, and while I have plenty of room for growth, I can manage longer stretches than before.

Sometimes holding on to God's presence as I go about my day is exhilarating, liberating, and even fun. I think God likes humor, music, creativity, working puzzles, and building beautiful things out of messes. I feel his pleasure in teaching me about his creation both in people and nature. He points out details, rhythms, and beauty. I'm reminded of the lyrics from an old hymn: "He walks with me and he talks with me." I feel he is ever happy to teach and show me the world.

Other times prayer is mundane, uneventful, and boring. Probably the hardest part about growing in deeper intimacy with God is that the feelings and senses visit and fade. Sometimes I'm left with an emptiness like no other. I'm left feeling vacant, and ordinary life fails to satisfy. I miss God. It's like visiting the neighborhood park after going to Disneyland. I guess I wouldn't miss him had I not experienced him.

The old writers would say his absence is a grace. It is out of love that he hides. We do well to remember that God's hiddenness can be helpful in the growth of our souls. God's absence is as much an act of love as his presence. It is in the lonely spaces where faith is forged.

I'm reminded again of trees and how they do most of their growth in winter, pushing their mass toward deeper water sources. Spring is the opportunity for the tree to proudly display its winter labor. I don't really want to acknowledge it, but the empty times are when the most growth has occurred for me. They've been my chance to show up, to continue on. The valleys are opportunities to live as I do on the mountaintops, offering love and grace even when I feel none. I'm not good at that. Yet I know this is where my soul is formed. Sometimes I get tired of being formed.

I'm a little uncomfortable admitting it, but in my twenty-odd years of trying to connect with God, I've developed a sort of yearning for the afterlife. Sometimes the longing to be in a place filled with God's presence is painful. Secretly I've cried tears to return home, to live in a place where love and goodness rule and where evil is silenced. Yet I'm committed to being here. In fact, since my experience with solitude in Virginia, I want to be in the here and now more than ever. It's a continual paradox.

As my experience with practicing the presence of God continues, I'm finding a deepening awareness of the way I view and treat others. God seems glad to reveal insight into their lives. The rude cashier at the grocery store turns into a wounded person spewing venom on anyone willing to take it. The guy who cuts me off in traffic is pitied for the frantic pace he lives. The woman scantily clad in inappropriate clothing is just baring a deep longing for a love she can't seem to find. It's easy to offer little prayers for people. Sometimes when I find myself bored, I turn to prayer. Waiting in line or sitting in a meeting, rather than staring at the clock, I begin to pray for people, secretly bombing those in the room with the love of the Father. I watch as smiles emerge or softness covers faces. It feels like magic, and it's fun.

Prayer is as much about listening as it is anything else. It's about being still. Sometimes I'll pray for hours and utter only a few words or none at all. It has become a series of gentle movements, of resting in the presence of God, a dance of sorts where my thoughts, will, and intentions meld with the presence of God. I'll seamlessly move from still-filled moments silently waiting, listening in a sort of meditative posture, to uttering a word or single sentence aloud. Sometimes I use a lot of words, but as I delve into this prayer-filled life, those times are becoming less and less frequent.

When I catch God's desires and intentions for others, prayer is like floating down a river with a swift current—movement is almost effortless. Yet other times prayer is paddling upstream, with no rhythm, requiring tremendous energy.

Sometimes our prayers for others, the little offerings we make, deplete our spiritual reserves, like when the woman desperate for healing touched the hem of Jesus's robe and he felt power go out from him.[4] And when the tank is empty, into the void of silence we must return.

A few years ago my wife and I faced a prolonged season of illness with our daughter. Things were bad and I was scared. I couldn't find the energy to really pray for her. I'd lay my hands on her while she slept, and I'd grunt, I'd groan, I'd whisper, "Please . . . help!" But beyond that, I just couldn't find the strength. So I'd light a candle and hope that my tears were enough.

"Dad, no words could come. I tried to pray and I just felt so helpless," I confessed.

"Oh, of course, Nate. We do what we can," he said sympathetically. "Prayer for healing takes great energy. Don't disregard the times when words won't come. The Spirit works with those grunts and groans. It's also at those times when the prayers of others carry us."

My mind returned to the image of the father waiting by the fence, suffering for his prodigal son.

I remember one day telling Bill about how I often saw deep hurt and pain in people's eyes. Sometimes in crowded places the worn faces filled with loss and heartache were overwhelming.

"Nate, God shows you that so you can pray for them," he told me.

"Bill, I can't pray for everyone. I'd be praying all the time."

"Exactly. You don't need to say anything," he stated, almost as if I was supposed to know it. "Just lift your hand up. You take the hurt you see and you lift it up to God." He waved his hand in an upward motion. "Just give it to him. He can hold it."

So this is what I did. And this is what I do when I see the hurt and pain in the world.

Bill spent the bulk of his career praying for others. People would come from all over the world to spend time with him. He was a kind, gentle man, an obsessive flirt, and a smiling jokester who loved well. On January 29, 2011, William Luther Vaswig, my father's closest friend for forty years and one of the most beautiful and childlike men I had ever known, died.

It was seven o'clock on a Sunday night when my dad called asking to practice reading the eulogy he would be delivering for Bill the following day. He was afraid he would choke up when he delivered it. I told him to choke up and not to fear public tears.

"Nate, I wish you could come. It's going to be a tough three days." His voice cracked.

Ten hours later, I was boarding a plane for Seattle, and that afternoon Dad and I sheepishly entered the mortuary for the viewing. No one else was there. Soft music poured from a monitor playing a continuous loop of pictures. A photo of my dad, Bill, and Dallas Willard flipped by. I smiled at the thought of these three great men hanging out together in the early 1970s. I wondered if they ever imagined the life they would each lead.

Sometimes my dad and Bill were embarrassing to be with in public. They liked to pretend Bill couldn't speak English, and my dad would translate in a made-up, unconvincing Norwegian accent. The practical jokes, the giggling, the dancing, the funny stories—the two of them together was a special sight. Sometimes we forget that saints laugh. Holy people are funny people.

"Nate, come here. Touch him. See, he's gone. He's not here," Dad whispered with a sincere smile.

Although it may seem hard to believe, this was the first time I had seen a dead body, let alone touched one, but my dad was having an important moment and I wanted to honor that, so I bit my lip and faced the corpse before me. What happened next was so strange I've found it hard to talk about. I hesitantly reached out to touch Bill's hand. As my skin touched his, something happened. Bill shocked me! In a spontaneous reaction, I jerked away slightly, trying not to alarm my dad. Electricity rung through my hand. It was like shaking hands with my son and his toy buzzer. I touched Bill again. This time I wasn't shocked, but I felt a hum of energy flowing from him. For ten minutes I held his hand, I cried, and I smiled as I felt his care for me.

For the next three days heat radiated from my hand. Occasionally it still returns. Even as I write this, months later, I feel this gentle buzzing. I always smile. I don't know what to make of it, but I figure I should use my buzzing hand to pray for people. I've always liked to lay hands on people and pray for them, yet I'm often too shy to ask. When I got home from Seattle, I had a message on my voice mail asking me to come teach a group on prayer. I've been asked to teach on a number of different topics, but never before on prayer. I said yes, just for Bill, with the condition that I could use some of my time to pray for the group. I gave the best lecture I could put together on prayer and then spent an hour laying my hands on each person. I prayed my heart out, went home, and simply went to bed.

I'll never forget Bill or standing graveside and listening to my father deliver the final words. I watched two of the graveyard workers appear from the hazy shadows with muddy clothes and long, greasy hair carelessly tucked under their hats. Both had a good two weeks' worth of facial stubble covering the scars of sadness and hope lost in days past. I imagine Bill would have loved to talk with these men. I could see him taking them in and praying for them with well-executed profanity and perfectly timed laughter. I watched as the workers nervously sauntered over to the casket, maneuvered ropes and hooks, and began to drop my friend's cold shell into the ground.

With an echoing thud, the earthly chapter was closed on eighty years of a life spent loving and praying. The earthly experience of William Luther Vaswig was to be no more. And while his memory, his goodness, his laughter, and his love will continue to reverberate for many years, I do not exaggerate when

I say his death was a profound loss for humanity. The heroes of our age are dying. But in death, God always seems to find a way to bring about new beginnings.

Prayer
Teresa of Avila (1515–1582)

Raised by a family of merchants, Teresa entered the Carmelite monastic order at age twenty. After twenty years in the order, she had what she called a second conversion. She compared this experience to that of Augustine in his *Confessions*. This conversion experience led her to be a key cog in the Roman Catholic counter-reformation and helped renew the church's focus on contemplation and Christian mysticism. In 1562, she founded St. Joseph's monastery in Avila. She spent the last twenty years of her life writing about and living out a life of contemplation and prayer.

In her autobiography, *The Life of Saint Teresa of Avila by Herself*, she identified four different states of prayer. The first she called "mental prayer" or "the first water."[5] She described this type of prayer as "drawing the water from the well by one's own control."[6]

Second, the "prayer of quiet" requires less effort by oneself. We have fewer distractions in this stage. At this stage, "the soul begins to lose desire for earthly things" and we begin "to come in contact with the supernatural."[7]

The third stage of prayer, "devotion of union," is when the Lord does the work and becomes the gardener of our soul. The soul "has done nothing except consent to the Lord's granting it graces, and embraces it with its will."[8]

Her final stage of prayer is the "devotion of ecstasy" in which there is no effort on our part whatsoever, only ecstasy. We are completely enraptured by the joining of God and human.

Teresa's autobiographical writings and life's work on prayer and mysticism are just as applicable and important to Christians today as they were in the sixteenth century.

Understanding
Guidance

In the Christian discipline of guidance, we are learning to live under the theocratic rule of God. This is no small task.

In the beginning we discover our will in opposition to and in struggle with the will of God. We want what we want when we want it. In time, however, we begin to see the goodness of rightness—that is, that God's will is not only right but altogether good. So there comes through time and experience—sometimes much time and experience—a releasing of our will and a flowing into the will of the Father. When this time comes, we desire more than any other thing to do the will of God. Hence, we are thrust into the lifelong task of learning the skills of guidance.

One of the very first things that occur through this learning process is that acquaintanceship with God gives way to friendship with God. In human relationships, close friends are easily able to distinguish the voices of one another over all others. So it is with God. Instinctively, we come to recognize the *quality* in the voice of God, for it is one of drawing and encouraging. We recognize the *spirit* in the voice of God, for it is full of grace and mercy. And we discover that the *content* of what is being said is always consistent with what God has said before. We have a huge biblical witness by which to test our leadings.

Then there comes to us a fuller understanding of the *means* of divine guidance. Most common to Christian believers is the direct revelation of the Holy Spirit upon the human heart. E. Stanley

Jones notes that the Holy Spirit "does not argue, does not try to convince you. It just speaks and it is self-authenticating."[1] In addition, the Christian community is given to us to help affirm and clarify any particular word we might receive from the Lord. Then too, it is helpful to consider the role of personal integrity in guidance. The wise writer of Proverbs says, "The integrity of the upright guides them."[2] Divine providence is yet another means of guidance, whereby God causes circumstances to work for his will. Of course, there is Holy Scripture, which shows us how God has worked in the past. "Your word is a lamp to my feet and a light to my path," says the psalmist.[3]

There are, to be sure, exceptional means of guidance. I am thinking here of such experiences as signs, visions, dreams, and angels. Such experiences do indeed happen and are at times used of God to guide his people. But, as I say, these are the "exceptional" means of guidance. The most common way God guides us is by means of the "still small voice" of the Spirit.

Jesus tells us that he is the Good Shepherd and that his sheep hear and know his voice.[4] What wonderful, good news! We have a divine Shepherd who is always with us: accepting us, forgiving us, teaching us, guiding us. This is the confidence we can have as we learn the ways and means of guidance.

Richard J. Foster

10

Guidance

Embracing the Desert

God made the desert so man can find his soul.

Anonymous

Toward the end of the third century, Christianity had become the state religion throughout much of Northern Africa. When religion becomes deeply ingrained in a culture, it doesn't take long for the faith to become diluted. Often within a generation or two you'll find people following the precepts more out of instinct or unconscious cultural pressure than genuine conviction. Then come the vultures, preying on the decaying scraps. The political machine smells power, and entrepreneurs eye money to be made. Same story as Judaism in the days of Moses and David; same as Christianity in our own. What was once a great movement of God calling his people home gives way to mass apathy and corruption.

Yet in spite of our human capacity to destroy good things, God continues to call, and new movements continue to spring forth. Around AD 300 in Northern Africa, God's voice of guidance led thousands of men and women to give their possessions away and move to the desert to embrace a life largely consisting of prayerful solitude.

The desert has often been a learning space for those seeking God. For those following the examples of Moses, Jesus, and John the Baptist, leaving home to train in the wild stillness of the sand was a little like us leaving home to study at a university.

Now, some were probably mentally ill, and likely some just wanted to avoid Roman taxes, but most felt guided by God, seeing the desert as training in godliness.[1] Known simply as the desert fathers and mothers, these humble people would become famous across the land for their insights and wisdom and would eventually birth what we now know as monasteries and convents. Their lives are preserved in a handful of wise and sometimes really bizarre sayings and stories.

What drew me to the desert fathers and mothers, other than the seeming madness of selling all your possessions for a celibate life of solitude in the hot desert, was their use of the spiritual disciplines, particularly the discipline of guidance. They used disciplines not only as a means of spiritual growth but as their tool to combat boredom, crankiness, the desire for comfort, or the urge to return to the cities.

Many of the fathers and mothers went to the desert to fight demons. Their stories are some of the strangest tales on spiritual warfare I have encountered, but what struck me was how they used the disciplines as their primary weapon.

For the early church, spiritual practices were much more integrated into who they were than we see today. People around the Middle East understood the power and freedom that come from training. It was common knowledge that the Greek athlete, whose body could respond to competition with grace and ease, only achieved that ability through the rigors of preparation. Physical training didn't have the same tone of drudgery as it does for us; getting to train was an honor and a luxury few were given the opportunity to experience. The idea of looking for shortcuts to become better or faster didn't seem to occur to them. It was simply a matter of putting in the effort and hours to develop a deeply ingrained habit so that when called upon, they could respond appropriately. So when Paul used the Greek word for Olympic training, *askesesiser*, when he said, "train yourself in godliness,"[2] this needed no explanation for the early Christians. If you want to become like Jesus, then you should train like Jesus and follow his examples of prayer, fasting, meditation, solitude, study, submission, and so on—the disciplines.

While the early church benefited from a deep understanding of the power of practicing the disciplines, I can't help but think that the desert fathers and mothers did seem to lack prudence. I'm not sure repeatedly doing long fasts and sleeping on a bed of rocks for fifteen years was exactly what Paul meant when he said to go train. Yet there is just too much insight and wisdom in their words to simply brush them off as crazy extremists. They were clearly on to something. They took the discipline of guidance to a level that would get many of us locked up in a mental institution.

One afternoon, in desert father fashion, I found myself leaning against a hot tree, repeatedly wiping the ants from my legs as I read about these men and women and their lives. These people viewed suffering as the road to peace and freedom. Jesus's words to take up your cross and follow me meant the Christian didn't need to run from suffering, but rather could view it as a refinement process. And like it or not, sometimes we are guided into suffering.

I fear the desert. I fear what I might find. I get the appeal of having a desert experience; an extended desert survival boot camp would be a cool accomplishment. But to voluntarily choose the desert life? Suffer for more than testing one's manhood or having an unusual experience that would make for a good story? Embracing suffering as medicine for my soul? I began to wonder about the little deserts we find ourselves in. The fathers and mothers went to the desert, but I wondered, does the desert sometimes find us? As an answer to my question, the voice of guidance came to my thoughts softly and clearly: "Embrace the desert." I knew it was a word from God; it had the texture of love and the tone resonated so deep within me that tears bubbled up. I wrote it down and went on with my day.

So often, in our need to work out our own experiences, we feel compelled to be the bearer of guidance or advice to others. Throughout the years I've found that whether it comes from God, another person, or a community, guidance that changes people's lives usually requires few words. As Henri Nouwen so effectively states, "Sometimes it seems that our many words are more an expression of our doubt than of our faith. It's as if we are not sure that God's Spirit can touch the hearts of people: we have to help him out and, with many words, convince others of his power. But it is precisely this wordy unbelief that quenches the fire."[3]

More often than not, the most powerful words of guidance are also words that we don't want to hear. Learning how, when, and whom to ask for guidance is painful but necessary in our growth. If you are lost on a mountain and come upon a sign, you feel relief in knowing you are no longer lost. However, you may now know you just went fifteen miles in the wrong direction and have a lot of work ahead.

Through the years I've experienced God's voice of guidance—leading, teaching, correcting. It's a subtle voice that reveals how present God is in my daily happenings. I never really thought about this as practicing a discipline, probably because it was something I wanted, needed, and felt lost without. I am beginning to believe I should start viewing the disciplines similarly, as a grace I need to live well.

There are countless ways to practice the discipline of guidance. My opportunity that day came from three simple words: "Embrace the desert."

Later that afternoon my sign appeared in the midst of an argument with my wife.

My wife has struggled with an autoimmune disease and has been sick in one way or another for the majority of our relationship. Trying to raise two kids with a sick wife and no family close by is a story in and of itself. With all the tests, hospital visits, tears, isolation, longing, and broken dreams, I sometimes think I could fill the pages of a book, except I don't remember most of it. A few years ago I was leafing through some old medical bills and found I had no recollection of the stories associated with the thousands of dollars spent. I've blocked it out. It's as if I used denial to deal with my wife being sick. I don't like to look at it. I don't want to admit how bad it has been. With a sort of cold detachment, I've navigated the crises and moved on. For the most part this has served me well.

Christy has fought desperately to get better, and in the last few years her efforts have finally paid off. She's even become a health coach and now helps others heal. But occasionally the pain and fatigue become too much. If she rests and doesn't try to do too much, she's usually better in a day or two. I try my best to be helpful. I've gotten used to putting everything on hold at a moment's notice and attempting to be a single dad. I don't think much about it. I don't like it. I feel sorry for her. I want the situation to go away. Denial.

Recently her pain returned after a two-year remission, and she had to spend a great deal of time bedridden.

I'm not sure what we were arguing about, but it was the usual fight. I felt I was being unfairly accused, so rather than listen, I crafted clever retorts and offered a litany of evidence as to why she was wrong, which of course only served to escalate the situation. At one point she paused, and with fire in her tear-stained eyes and a piercingly pointed finger, she prophetically let loose.

"You can't handle it when I'm sick. It scares you. You can't do anything about it, so you check out. You get cold and distant. I need you to be with me. I'm suffering. I need you to not check out!"

She was right. I think on any other day her words would have been lost in my entitlement and my resentment about all I had done. But that day I heard it. It was clear: this was my desert to embrace.

Through the years I had shown up—I had cooked and cleaned, taken care of the kids, and made many a midnight run to the store—but emotionally, when she was sick, I checked out. When my wife suffered, I went into survival mode and did the tasks that had to be done, sometimes with a good attitude, often with brewing resentment. It was often duty or necessity that drove me, not love.

If my goal in life is to love well, then the opportunity to do so was right in front of me.

The voice of guidance was teaching me a new way to live.

As soon as I began to emotionally connect with Christy in her illness, a flood of realizations came. I couldn't fix her. I had no answers to soothe my fears. I quickly discovered that denial had served to block out a whole mess of worry and sadness. When I sat with her emotionally, I had to confront the reality that I had married a woman who was chronically ill. I felt so isolated and alone in this struggle. Her illness was invisible and very difficult to understand, let alone explain, so through the years I'd hardly tried to explain it to even my closest friends. Facing her illness meant acknowledging that for one reason or another my family, friends, and community hadn't showed up through our years of need. In part this was probably due to my lack of communication, but even still, some didn't want to know or seem to care.

This hurt. We all have such a huge capacity for selfishness, yet I'm sure some were probably feeling fear and using denial to deal with our situation in the same way I had been.

As I embraced my desert and the uncomfortable emotions, I felt exposed and vulnerable. In God's tender care I sensed a gentle nudge to carve out extra space for quiet and solitude. I began walking and taking a little bit of time to read and journal every day. This became an opportunity to process all the junk I had hidden away. God is so wonderful at bringing things together mysteriously, paradoxically, in such right and beautiful ways. I feel his pleasure in guiding us on journeys filled with twists and turns, plots and endings that are creatively ingenious. The discipline of guidance had led me to suffer, which drew me to care for someone I loved, but ultimately his voice led to my own healing. A paradox of love.

I want to tell you that in the days that followed, I was fully present to my wife in her illness. I wasn't. Deeply ingrained habits are hard to break. Emotionally it was exhausting; the more I tried to connect with her, the more I suffered. But as I watched her health recover, I made a commitment to stay in this process and at least try to see the desert as helpful in the formation of my soul.

I know this sounds weird, but through this experience I began to feel that God was more concerned about me and who I was becoming than about my happiness. I felt that his love for me extended far beyond my temporal comfort and what I thought I wanted. In his gentle embrace, suffering could be okay, a means to an end. I began trying to see it as a friend, or perhaps a teacher.

Through this project, the exact practice of each discipline was surprisingly turning out to be something highly individualized. I was beginning to become increasingly uninterested in uniform and specific ways to approach the spiritual life. I was reminded of the dangers of turning the disciplines into a to-do list. After all, connection with God is probably the most intimate and personal thing we ever do. So I assume the discipline of guidance is practiced differently for everyone. It seems all that's needed is space to listen and then taking action. The Bible is filled with stories of God using all sorts of means to speak. His guidance so beautifully comes through thoughts, a book, or another person, and each word is highly personal and unique. I wonder if he reserves an audible voice as a final means to get our attention.

Once again, the lines between specific disciplines were blurring and opportunities to practice each one were continuing to present themselves. Guidance was leading me to learn to suffer well.

Last Christmas Eve I came down with a stomach virus. At the visitors' center of Muir Woods in Northern California is a really cool wooden carving of a life-sized bear cub. I clung to its neck while I violently vomited all over its backside. The drive back to my hotel was one of the worst hours of my life.

As I curled up in the fetal position in my hotel bed, shivering under five thick blankets, it occurred to me that it was of no use to fight my illness. I would most likely spend the next twenty-four hours vacillating between shivering and sweating profusely while periodically racing to the bathroom, and there was nothing I could do about it. I thought about the desert fathers and embracing the deserts I found myself in. I thought about finding freedom when I submit. So as I lay in a hotel room with a shirt covered in vomit, I wondered, "What would happen if I let go? What if I didn't fight the pain and just submitted to my illness?" I listened to my body and relaxed. I even smiled.

I began to realize that the chills, stomach pain, and throwing up were the result of my body trying to heal itself. My body was only responding as God had programmed it to do when a virus attacks. I began to think of my throwing up as a gift from God. God was healing me. And in the midst of my misery, I found an opportunity to worship. As I write about it now, it sounds crazier than it felt in the moment, but I began to pray: "Thank you. . . . Oh, let the pain be my teacher." And so the next time I ran to the bathroom, I strongly whispered, "Yes! Bring it on! Heal me!"

The next morning was Christmas. I awoke, took a shower, and lay on my brother's couch the entire day, with a big goofy grin of gratitude.

Having a stomach virus is just awful, but there was something glorious about this experience. It felt good to accept that I don't always have to have control. Though my sickness only lasted a day, I was able to accept the process and suffer well.

I have since found a new respect for those who are forced to live lives of constant pain and suffering. And much like I've seen in my wife, I believe the years can bring a depth, a formation, like nothing else.

Life is a series of unfamiliar paths. We take new jobs and make moves. We navigate marital, parenting, and relational challenges. And as we age, we face a whole new set of issues both socially and physically. All while the car breaks down, the toilet backs up, we get the flu, and our neighbor's dog keeps pooping in our yard.

Just when we get comfortable in one season of life, a new one is being ushered in. Life brings constant unfamiliarity and with it the reality that so often we don't have any clue how to best address and traverse the struggles we face. We try. We fail. And the unfamiliar path continues.

Intrinsically indicative of the human experience is our aloneness. While I've grown to value the people in my life as some of the greatest gifts ever, no matter how connected we are, in the end, in the dead of night, we are alone. Trying to escape this fact motivates much of our destructive human behavior.

Then along comes Jesus, vowing to never leave us or forsake us, which almost seems flippant with no visual, physical, or even auditory evidence of his presence. Still, something profoundly changes when I tune in to his promise. I sit. I listen. "You're here, right? You'll help, right?" My task is not to make God show up but to patiently wait, fully expecting, fully anticipating some form of awareness that he is truly with me.

While active realization of his presence is welcomed and a great joy, I'm continuing to learn that his absence is also a gift, an act of love, and a means of my movement toward Christian maturity. Last year as I wept bitter tears, a word came to me: "Your lack is your teacher. Be thankful for good instructions— good opportunities to grow."

The expectant longing and the ache of anticipation have the potential to begin healing the core brokenness of my soul that fears aloneness. In this place we learn the utter beauty of arms raised to the sky crying, "'Eli, eli, lama sabachthani?' that is, 'My God, my God, why have you forsaken me?'"[4]

In this end, the mysterious paradox begins to reveal itself. Our bottom may be the only place where we can deeply know that we are never, never, never alone.

Guidance
Frank Laubach (1884–1970)

Born in Pennsylvania, Laubach studied at Princeton University, Columbia University, and Union Theological Seminary. He was ordained as a minister in 1914 and served as a missionary first in the Philippines and later in India.

He became known for his writings on prayer and mysticism and his "Each One Teach One" literacy campaign.

Laubach's goal of constant communication with God was marked by his two main purposes: to try to do God's loving will for him, continually, and to try to think God's thoughts continually. In this relentless communication, God guided Laubach in his literacy work in the early 1930s, which would eventually teach 60 million people worldwide how to read in their own respective languages.

While championing the cause of literacy, he still maintained a focus on God, specifically prayer. He authored many books reflecting on the presence of God. He tried to take seriously the scriptural call to "pray without ceasing."[5] In a short booklet, *The Game with Minutes*, he challenged Christians to focus on God "one second out of every sixty minutes."

Laubach once described the teaching of literacy as "the romance of opening blind eyes." It was this passion for teaching literacy to the developing world and respecting others in his missionary work that led to outside recognition of his work. Gandhi noted Laubach as someone he admired. President Harry Truman was influenced by Laubach to improve the developing world. On the one hundredth anniversary of his birth, Laubach became the only American missionary to be honored on a United States postage stamp.

Understanding

Worship

Worship is our human response to God's divine initiative.

Think of Isaiah in the splendor of Solomon's temple, experiencing the astonishing vision of the Lord high and lifted up. The temple is filled with a myriad of angels flying around and calling out to one another, "Holy, holy, holy is the Lord of hosts; the whole earth is full of his glory." The foundations of the temple begin to shake and the whole place is filled with heavenly smoke. No wonder Isaiah cries out, "Woe is me! I am lost, for I am a man of unclean lips, and I live among a people of unclean lips: yet my eyes have seen the King, the Lord of hosts!"[1]

Or think of John on the barren island of Patmos "in the spirit on the Lord's day."[2] He hears a booming voice like a trumpet, and he sees seven golden lampstands with the resurrected Jesus in the middle, clothed in a long robe with a golden sash. Jesus's hair is like a blizzard of white, his eyes like a flame of fire, his feet like furnace-fired bronze, and his voice like the sound of many waters. He holds seven stars in his hand, out of his mouth comes a razor-sharp sword, and his face shines like the blazing sun of noonday. No wonder John "fell at his feet as though dead."[3]

What an explosion of supernatural sound and color and image and energy! Who wouldn't fall to the ground in the face of such staggering divine initiatives?

But most of us must admit that these are not *our* normal experiences when we shuffle off to our local church. There the drums are too loud, the person next to us sings off-key, and we fight to stay awake through the sermon. Even when we wander into the magnificent granite cathedrals of nature, we struggle, for the sun is too hot and the mosquitoes bite.

Our efforts at worship certainly seem rather ordinary when compared with Isaiah and John. Perhaps we feel like we are stuck in the outer court when everyone else has gone into the inner court and a select few have entered the holy of holies.

Still, we should not despise our seemingly feeble efforts at worship. God is with us. Who knows when the divine initiative may come to fan the coals of our worship into a burning blaze? George Fox counseled, "Meet together in the Name of Jesus . . . he is your prophet, your shepherd, your bishop, your priest, in the midst of you, to open to you, and to sanctify you, and to feed you with life, and to quicken you with life."[4]

So whether our worship experience is of the fireworks variety of Isaiah and John or of a more ordinary kind, we can all follow the wise counsel of the apostle Paul: "Let the word of Christ dwell in you richly; teach and admonish one another in all wisdom; and with gratitude in your hearts sing psalms, hymns, and spiritual songs to God."[5] Then, in the presence of God the prayer of our hearts can be simply, "Set my spirit free, that I may worship Thee."

Richard J. Foster

11

Worship

Responding to the Divine Spark

Worship is our response to the overtures of love from the heart of the Father. Its central reality is found "in spirit and truth." It is kindled within us only when the Spirit of God touches our human spirit. Forms and rituals do not produce worship, nor does the disuse of forms and rituals. We can use all the right techniques and methods, we can have the best possible liturgy, but we have not worshiped the Lord until Spirit touches spirit.

Richard J. Foster[1]

I don't really like the word *worship*. It's one of those antiquated words that people throw around to describe an event or style of music. I don't think we actually mean "worship" when we say the word. We use it more as a noun than a verb.

Worship simply means to give worth, love, and admiration to someone or something. Of course, it's easy to attend a "worship service" or sing "worship music" and be far from actually worshiping, just like it's easy to give God, people, or things worth, love, and admiration outside of an official worship gathering. While worship is certainly not confined to gatherings or music, this seems to be the only intentional space in which we think to do it.

Worship comes in many forms. God initiates and we respond. When music sparks the love of God within us, we sing. When nature speaks to our heart, we give thanks, we show our adoration, we acknowledge God and his beauty. Prayer, fasting, and meditation allow us to tune in. Submission, service, confession, and simplicity create a humble posture. Study teaches us how to tap into the frequency of gratitude. Guidance shows us where to find God. We become aware, we respond, and a relationship is created and nurtured. This is how we learn we are loved. This is how we grow spiritually.

I find space for worship in lots of places: church, nature, at home alone. Sometimes for me it's as simple as an AA meeting or tucking my kids into bed. If worship is simply our response to God reaching out to us, then can we not carry this posture into almost everything we do?

My wife is an amazing singer-songwriter. After laying her music aside for years while she stayed home with the kids, her time recently came to step back out. She started singing and playing guitar at church and joined a classic rock cover band as their singer. As I continued to learn to play bass guitar, in the back of my mind was the idea for Christy to have her own band, one where she could play her songs and fully express her musical talent. I practiced virtually every day for months. Eventually, I achieved what I thought was impossible: I got good enough to start playing her songs. Soon after we started our own alternative rock band, Christy and The Professors.

Not only was playing music a hobby for us to do together, but it created space for her to live out the gifts God has given her. When we play, it's like I've never seen her before—she comes alive! On more than one occasion I've shivered in awe and delight at the beauty and power that come from her songs as she pours out the goodness she's kept locked inside all these years. God's Spirit touches her spirit, and she responds. Worship.

⁂

Once again, when I turned my intention toward a discipline, God seemed so graciously eager to join me on this journey of cultivating the growth of my soul.

Just as our band was forming, I was asked to play on a church worship team. I probably should have declined; practicing the same songs over and over with Christy was one thing, but to play new music each week on a stage was really beyond my ability. But hey, what better way to practice the discipline of worship?

For the first dozen Sundays I was so caught up in trying to make sure I played the right notes that I'm not sure I would say my playing had anything to do with worship. But as I began to feel more comfortable with what I was doing, I found I could get lost in actively responding to God in the music. Yet at these times, I found, I made mistakes.

A friend of mine who used to be a worship pastor offered some helpful thoughts. He used to view Sunday worship as performance. He was a perfectionist with how he played. He said perfectionism was his addiction, and people would praise him for this addiction. It wasn't until he learned to let go during worship that he understood that the best way to lead worship is to worship. Who cares if you mess up? Quit playing and get on your knees. It's not perfect music that draws people in; it's creating a space for God.

His words were helpful, as is being a part of a worship team that doesn't really care if you make mistakes. I stopped looking to create complex bass lines and became content to play simple notes while I set my heart on the act of worship. Now I close my eyes. I sing along. I respond with the plucking of my strings. What I've found most touching to me about the whole experience is looking out at the people and seeing looks of gratitude and heartache, a person crying in the corner, a man on his knees in the back, unnoticed, pleading for help. While I thump out the notes, I pray. I picture the Spirit falling on people, touching their concerns and joys.

While I have my concerns and complaints about institutionalized religion, the church does hold the possibility of being an honest community of broken people trying to be present to God and each other. I hate how dehumanizing business principles of growth and success have weaseled their way into American churches. I hate when it turns into a fake, theatrical show with more focus on being entertained or listening to an articulate, charismatic figure than on creating space for God. God's patience for such nonsense amazes me. Still, religious gatherings have the potential to join us together and to encourage, enrich, and instruct us in deeper things—to help us know and be known. We worship in those often fleeting moments when we pause long enough from the distractions of life and are able to place worth and value on God. Sometimes when I play during a service, I find myself strangely moved toward others. We share a space together, and I'm left with a connection to them. I find myself interested in people's lives, wanting to help and care for them, even those I've never talked to before.

Since biblical times, people have been writing about formal gatherings of the church as the highlight of their week. Historically, many people have risked their lives to be a part of corporate worship. I wish I understood that conviction. I love this line from Thomas Kelly describing his church experience: "wrapped in a sense of unity and of Presence such as quiets all words and enfolds us within an unspeakable calm and interconnectedness within a vaster life."[2] I want to go to his church. Just what drove people of the past and still moves many in other countries to put their lives on the line in order to gather? What am I missing? It must have been something more substantive than a slick production or the liturgies filled with strange customs and culturally irrelevant traditions that we find today.

Recently I've been drawn back to my Quaker heritage. I'm taken by the notion of viewing church business as an act of worship. Decision making is as much a part of their spiritual life together as any other activity. The focus is to create space for God to speak. The Quakers believe that because all can hear from God, it's possible for the group to be of one mind on matters of the community. By creating the space and time for consciousness to happen, they make this part of their worship. While this process can be annoying and painfully slow, the results are staggering. Quakers are the only denomination, to my knowledge, that has consistently been on the right side of history regarding social issues. This prayerful practice of collectively listening to the voice of Jesus guiding his community before making any decisions is what brought the Quakers to free all their slaves and pay them recompense over a hundred years before slavery was abolished in the United States. Quakers were on the front lines working and advocating for the poor, for women's right to vote, and for civil rights. This speaks to the power of a community seeking the voice of God as an act of their worship, rather than following the traditional church organization methods of allowing a select few in authority to make decisions.

Worship can have powerful results, far beyond singing a song and having an emotional experience. The fruit of our worship has the potential to shape the future of humankind.

While I've been growing in my appreciation of organized worship, the easiest venue for me to appreciate and adore God is in reading the first great book: the book of nature. So to continue practicing the discipline of worship, I went camping.

It had been a rough night in the little cave I'd slept in. The ground was bumpy and angled at a slope. The allure of spending a night sleeping in a Rocky Mountain cave had seemed worth the inconvenience. But I hadn't anticipated the hours would be filled with sleepy visions of a lost bear stumbling upon my borrowed patch of earth. I don't think I'll ever sleep in a cave again.

It was a Sunday morning, and all around the world countless faithful sheep were stumbling into sanctuaries with worn hope and the fresh wounds of the week's chaos. I thought of them as I knelt beside my little fire and brewed my morning coffee.

It was just before dawn; all the forest creatures knew it. Some softly scurried about their morning activities, trying not to disturb the quiet hush of the approaching sunrise; others lay waiting in anticipation.

The chorus always begins with that impatient bird that can no longer contain its enthusiasm and ignites the morning chirping. Little by little the whole choir of birds joins in, welcoming a new day in harmonious procession, declaring with all the beauty they can muster with their tiny breath that the world is bathed in the joy and love of God.

All around me, God's great book of creation was being preached.

I gently listened to the poetic growl of a distant river that flowed all day and night, never taking a holiday off. It echoed God's faithfulness.

I watched the trees dance in the breeze, and I thought of how important it is to be flexible if I'm to follow the ebbs and flows of the Spirit.

I observed a spider race across his web toward a recent catch, and I thought of the oppression and devastation that mark so many people's daily lives.

I examined a newly sprouted flower, and I was reminded that beauty is everywhere if only I take the time to find it.

I listened for the rocks to cry out in praise. I didn't hear anything. But I remembered the importance of being steadfast and solid in my gratitude—that my quality of life often hinges on being thankful for today's breath and for the people, things, and insights that I have and don't have.

A fluttering butterfly reminded me of the resilience, uniqueness, and creativity of others.

A hawk submitted to the wind and majestically soared, and I remembered the freedom I feel when I let go of trying to have my own way.

I studied the plants, grass, and trees scattered about in a chaotic fashion and remembered that in the chaos of life, God remains in the business of making beautiful landscapes out of our messes.

And as my Sunday service concluded, I breathed the morning air, a symbol that every day is a new chance to begin again.

After most worship services I attend, I don't remember the message and I leave with a familiar blend of longing and frustration, feeling lost in the mystery of God incarnate, confused by the human experience and the little symbols and traditions we use to try to remember and connect. I cling to faith that maybe one day it will all make sense. When church is at its best, I'm reminded that I'm not alone in this journey, and I feel connected to my community both locally and historically. Most helpful is when I walk out with a vague sense of hope and a bouquet of inspiration to love those around me. And that's how I left the woods that day. Oh, and of course, after church I'm always hungry and craving more coffee—that day was no different.

For this book project, I had grand plans to take my family on a road trip to Kansas City to visit a church I've heard has kept twenty-four-hour-a-day worship services going for years. I wanted to teach my kids, give them a cool experience practicing the discipline of worship. While I'm sure this would have been helpful, it spoke to my desire to go extreme with the disciplines, as well as my hidden belief that God would only show up in big situations. The truth is, God doesn't need big in order to show up. In fact, I think he'd rather us notice him showing up in everyday, mundane life. I'm learning to let go of the "bigger is always better" lie.

Being that nature has been such a special place for me to respond to God, I figured I should teach what I know. I decided to walk with my daughter on an old railroad trail near my house.

As we rested on a bench, stillness overtook us. After a good five minutes, Autumn broke the silence.

"Wow, Dad, that was amazing. I heard the branches creaking, a little bird fluttering, and the leaves blowing. Let's be quiet some more and listen."

So we did.

"Dad, can you believe God made all this? It's so perfect. So peaceful and right."

Worship.

Worship
John Muir (1838–1914)

John Muir immigrated to the United States with his family from Scotland at the age of eleven. He was raised by Protestant parents; his father was a stern man who used Scripture and physical punishment to raise his children. His father required him to memorize Scripture every day with the threat of physical abuse if he failed to do so. Muir memorized the entire New Testament and most of the Old Testament by the age of eleven. The Muir household was led with a tyrannical view toward work. The children were never even allowed to rest in the shade or take a break for a drink of water.

While in college at the University of Wisconsin, Muir was introduced to Christians with a much higher view of nature than the Christianity he was accustomed to. In 1867, Muir took a journey through the American South and on to California. It was on this journey that he encountered God's beauty through creation and experiencing the natural world became a spiritual and worshipful experience. Muir moved to Yosemite to experience God's creation. Even after he moved away to the San Francisco area, he returned to Yosemite often. He also took many journeys to experience God's natural world beyond the High Sierra mountains.

Muir viewed nature as God's sanctuary: "the hills and groves were God's first temples, and the more they are cut down and hewn into cathedrals and churches, the farther off and dimmer seems the Lord himself."[3] For Muir, being in nature, experiencing the wonder of God's creation, was an act of worship.

At the encouragement of friends, Muir began to publish articles on his experiences in nature. This led to a lifetime advocating for the protection and conservation of natural areas in the United States. Muir's activism and writings were an impetus for the creation of the country's national parks. He was the founder of the Sierra Club and became a fore-father of modern American environmentalism.

Understanding
Celebration

The spiritual discipline of celebration leads us into a perpetual jubilee of the Spirit. We are rejoicing in the goodness and the greatness of God. As Saint Augustine said, "The Christian should be an alleluia from head to foot."[1]

Celebration comes to us as the result of all the spiritual disciplines having done their work in our lives. The desired goal of the spiritual disciplines is to produce in us a deep character formation. The fruit of the Spirit *is* the "holy habits" of a truly formed life. In greater and deeper measure our life is being penetrated throughout by "love, joy, peace, patience, kindness, generosity, faithfulness, gentleness, and self-control."[2]

This deep-rooted character formation brings balance to our lives. Anger, bitterness, resentment, rancor, hostility, deceit—these things simply do not have the same control over us that they once did. We feel the impact of this in all our relationships: with our spouse, with our children, with our co-workers, with our neighbors, with our friends. Even with our enemies.

When the substance of our life is formed and conformed and transformed into Christlikeness, then celebration becomes possible. No longer do we undermine or sabotage the good work of God. We can simply and joyfully celebrate the goodness of God in us and in those around us. Celebration is made possible as the common ventures of life are redeemed.

Joy is at the heart of celebration. Indeed, I rather imagine it's the engine that keeps the entire operation going. "The joy of the

LORD is your strength," declared Nehemiah.[3] And so it is. Without joy penetrating all the disciplines, they will quickly deteriorate into another set of soul-killing legalisms.

Perhaps the most important benefit of celebration is that it saves us from taking ourselves too seriously. It is an occupational hazard of devout folk to become stuffy bores. Celebration delivers us from such a fate. It adds a note of gaiety, festivity, and hilarity to our lives.

Celebration gives us perspective on ourselves. We are not nearly as important as we often think we are, and celebration has a way of bringing us the needed balance. The high and the mighty and the weak and the lowly all celebrate together. Who can be high or low at the festival of God? Together the rich and the poor, the powerful and the powerless all share in the goodness of God. There is no leveler of caste systems like festivity.

Celebration is not just an attitude but also something that we do. We laugh. We sing. We dance. We play. The psalmist described the joy-filled celebration of the people of God complete with timbrel and dance, with trumpet and lute and harp, with strings and pipe and loud clashing cymbals. In celebration we celebrate!

Celebration is one of those things that does not diminish with use. Rather it multiplies. Celebration begets more celebration. Joy begets more joy. Laughter begets more laughter. I have found that times of genuine celebration have the potential of bringing healing and wholeness to the entire community. So . . . let's celebrate!

Richard J. Foster

12

Celebration

Tattooed Joy

> Joy is the most infallible sign of the presence of God.
>
> Léon Bloy[1]

Celebration is a loaded word. I can't seem to shake the image of giddy middle school girls or awkward parties where people embarrassingly try to make fun happen. I'm much more comfortable with deep conversation and a melancholy documentary. I more naturally find beauty in sadness than fun in social events. I'm an introvert, a tortured artist of sorts; parties just make me nervous. Back in high school I couldn't even bring myself to take my girlfriend, now my wife, to prom. This has always bothered me.

Even though I like holidays and celebrations, my fear and negativity have the potential to taint events. Birthdays can be an illustration that getting to have my way never really works out. Christmas can be an opportunity to be reminded that people don't really know much about me or what I want. Formal get-togethers are often clouded by my social anxiety or the fear of the attention they might bring. I know I'm a bit dramatic, but my tendency to focus on the negative and disappointments has been a real problem for me when it comes to celebrating.

In one sense my life has been marked by years of chasing one thing after another. The isolation, the longing, unfulfilled hope, and broken dreams; always searching, always eyeing the next mountain, greener pastures kind of stuff; never living in the moment and continually wondering what lies ahead. However wonderful the future turns out to be, it comes with new challenges. I'm often left wondering if I'm really going anywhere. I'm left tired and questioning if this is really all there is to life. Paul's invaluable secret of how to be content in any situation has frustrated and taunted me. Contentment never seems to last. And I've bought the lie that if only things come together, if only I have this job, or finish this project, or live in this house, or make this move, or have this paycheck, or buy this, or accomplish that, or when the kids get older—only then will I be happy. My hopes and desires betray me with a false sense of what they could bring.

Emptiness is always the result when chasing after the wind. I think I relate more to Solomon's ode to meaninglessness than I do to Paul's little secret. Yet I'm also finding something freeing in the meaninglessness of life. What really does matter? Am I becoming someone who loves well? Am I becoming someone who wants to be in heaven? The hollowness of life and its barrenness, which used to drive me into sadness and depression, now drive me toward God's kingdom. What's left other than love? C. S. Lewis's words in *Mere Christianity* are so helpful here: "If I find in myself a desire which no experience in this world can satisfy, the most probable explanation is that I was made for another world."[2]

I wonder if I have a habit of sabotaging good in my life. It was no coincidence that I saved the discipline of celebration for the last chapter.

I was surprised, and a bit relieved, to hear my father's description of celebration as a natural result of practicing the disciplines.

With each discipline we become more aware, more able to live in the moment, more capable of handling what life throws at us, more accepting of not getting our own way. We become balanced and content. And then *bam!* It happens: joy sneaks its way in. Celebration is a road to contentment and joy, which has more to do with gratitude, laughter, and a life free of cares than with some emasculated Santa or forced party.

My dad described celebration as not only the joy and contentment that result from a spiritually formed life but also something that can be practiced. In *Celebration of Discipline* he listed a few ways to intentionally practice celebration, but again, it was clear, there is no well-formulated way to go about the practice. Just like with the other disciplines, I was free to be myself and explore without the constraints of matching the experiences of others.

I want to be better at celebrating. Whether it's talked about or not, Jesus did set a precedent for a celebratory life. Why else would he attend the wedding in Cana? His teachings are laced with humor. Dad once told me he would love to see a painting of the disciples on a hill, sitting around a campfire, with Peter rolling on the ground laughing at a joke Jesus told.

I was ready to let go and celebrate. So, with intentionality intact, I waited for an opportunity to present itself.

It was May, and my university's annual faculty awards were being announced at chapel. Filled with grace and goodness, I successfully exchanged my usual feeling of desire and impending jealousy for fervent prayers for the joy the award would provide to someone else besides me. The students of my university voted and decided that a high school dropout, plagued with low self-esteem and a learning disability, should be the recipient of the teaching excellence award. My prayers went unanswered. I won.

Here I had given up needing, and even wanting, the award or the approval and had been praying for someone else to have it—and then I won. What fun! In letting go I received; the fruit of submission, service, and prayer. While I was uncomfortable with the attention, I wore my medal, got my picture taken, and took the family to a fancy restaurant. I celebrated. I didn't sabotage. It was good.

Enjoying this celebratory moment got me thinking about an upcoming event. It had been ten years since I'd had a drink or drug. This has been one of the most difficult things I have ever done in my life, but it's also allowed me to live and to have the life, people, and opportunities that I now have. I'm sure if I had not gotten sober, things would have turned out very differently, very badly. The anniversary of my ten years of sobriety seemed like a great time to practice celebration.

As it turned out, the day before my anniversary, my family was driving home from a physically and emotionally exhausting, one-month, seven-state trip working and visiting family, so we decided to postpone the celebration until we returned. However, while driving home, I got this idea that I wanted to buy a kayak and spend the afternoon exploring the coves and marshes of a nearby lake. I immediately let Christy know about my plans. She thought it might be best to rent one to try out since I had some back problems and had never actually been in a kayak. All she really wanted was to make sure it wouldn't reinjure my back. I took this as my cue to sabotage the whole event. And so, for the next three hundred miles, spanning three states and six hours, we unleashed on each other our frustration about the heat, the lack of sleep, and the irritations of the trip. In traditional sabotaging fashion, I spent the next day sulking and refused to allow her to acknowledge my accomplishment. No kayak was rented or purchased. No celebration occurred. Bitterness won.

As I looked for another chance to work on celebration, again the prospect found me. Christy was turning forty and decided she wanted a party, a big party. I wanted more than anything to give her what she desired. But I was intimidated. Christy grew up Jehovah's Witness and didn't get to celebrate birthdays, and this only added to the pressure. I tried not to think about this as a chance to fail, but I did. Enlisting the help of some friends, I went all out: cool invitations, food, decorations, and the perfect venue. We decided to have our band play because, as Christy says, "Forty rocks!" It was a great celebration. Christy was in her element with a guitar strapped to her and her passion pouring into the mic. The night was fun. It was a celebration. I had done well.

I'm unsure what exactly motivated me to question her gratitude a couple of days later, but I did. Christy was extremely appreciative and even said it was the best fortieth party she could have ever hoped for. Even still, I proceeded to taint yet another celebration with a lengthy argument.

I certainly need more practice with celebration, although I'm learning. My insecurities and self-doubt are what keep me from joy. God accepts me; therefore, I can accept myself. God doesn't shame me; I don't need to shame myself. I'm free to let others accept, reject, or judge me. As my dad has said, "Freedom from anxiety and care forms the basis of celebration."[3]

As with the other disciplines, maybe it would have been better to start with small celebrations rather than just going for the big events, like starting by fasting for one day instead of ten. Could I be intentional and find joy in my daily life?

Sometimes daily, but at least a few times per week, I've started going on walks with my daughter. I listen intently as she spouts Harry Potter trivia or the plotline to some *Doctor Who* episode, which often leads to her letting me in on her life and the struggles of being a thirteen-year-old girl. We laugh at puns and talk about physics. We still listen to the leaves and birds. She has helped me work out situations and make decisions. I like her. It feels good to be a dad. Our walks are a really simple act, but it feels like a moment of holy celebration in the midst of the ordinary.

We signed my son up for Cub Scouts, and I decided to become a leader. His excitement to earn badges is contagious. Helping him accomplish his goals almost feels better than meeting goals myself. We also spend time playing video games together. When there is a level he can't get through, he turns to me, and vice versa. I wrestle with him. He thinks I'm cool. I think he's cool. Joy.

When my birthday rolled around this year, I decided to deal with my joy sabotage by giving the day to my kids. With a little more guidance than the day I gave to them while practicing submission, I let them choose the restaurant, the type of cake, and the activity we did. Best birthday ever.

Celebrating in little ways helps. The small, simple joys feel easy. It's here that I'm able to approach life as living in God's smile.

I'm now wondering if celebration could be a chance to turn a regret into something wonderful. The other day I found an ad for a prom for married couples. My wife and I are so going—fancy clothes, corsage, and maybe even a limo.

Remember the Martin Luther King Jr. quote my daughter adapted? Last year I had the phrase tattooed on my arm: "I decided to choose love." It serves as a reminder that in the end, no matter how difficult, I will choose love. Anger, bitterness, and hatred are not the path I will walk down. When I got this tattoo, I knew it would be significant. But I really had no idea how much it would change me. I have to look at this phrase every single day. If I'm in a bad mood or if I'm mad at someone or about something and I see the tattoo, it helps me stop and think about the choices I'm making.

This journey of practicing the disciplines brought an idea for a beautiful but emotionally difficult commitment. What if, on my other arm, I got another tattoo saying "I decided to choose joy"?

I asked Christy her opinion.

"I would so love it!" was her excited reaction. She knows better than anyone the impact the last tattoo had on me.

And with a tear in her eye and hopeful anticipation, she sheepishly asked, "Are you willing to commit to joy like that? Really?"

Celebration
Saint Francis of Assisi (1181–1226)

Born into a family of wealthy merchants in Assisi, Italy, Francis spent a short time as a soldier and working for his father's business. Responding to the call of an "inner voice," he decided to leave his old life of wealth and repair the ruined church of San Damiano. He was said to have sung at the top of his voice while restoring the church. For many years he lived alone as a beggar to identify with the poor. Gradually others gathered around Francis and joined this lifestyle. In 1210, he drew up a rule of life and had it approved by Pope Innocent III. The group following this rule called themselves "friars." Francis traveled throughout Europe preaching. During this time the group grew to five thousand members. Francis lived out the remaining years of his life humbly, holding no official position and living quietly within the order.

Often we hear stories of the lengths Francis went to in order to refrain from sinful thoughts, including putting dirt in his food (so as not to enjoy the taste), jumping in a cold stream when he felt sexual impulses, or choosing to live the impoverished life. Francis celebrated the poor and poverty itself.

He is considered the first to have celebrated Christmas with a nativity scene. He often celebrated the beauty of God's creation in song (Pope John Paul II even named him the Patron Saint of Ecology) and according to legend would preach to the birds of the air. He even found joy in suffering: "We must rejoice when we would fall into various trials and endure every sort of anguish of soul and body or ordeals in this world for the sake of eternal life."[4]

For Francis, life in Christ was a celebration to be lived, and he is often quoted as saying, "Preach the gospel always—if necessary, use words."

Conclusion

Endings and New Beginnings

All shall be well, and all shall be well, and all manner
of thing shall be well.

Julian of Norwich[1]

It is often the case in life that my growth happens while I'm
looking the other direction. Like watching a little seed, I don't
necessarily notice any sprouting, and then one day the forest is
alive. Our development is slow and persistent, similar to that
of God's other creations, the earth and the planets.

As I now reflect on the past four years, I see that joy has
sprouted.

I no longer see the disciplines as something unattainable,
reserved for the super spiritual or stuffy monkish folks. Practicing the disciplines rather feels like a gentle and graceful attune-
ment to seeking God in the everyday mess and simple things.
Sometimes it's as easy as being thoughtful and intentional in
my actions, unafraid to try new things. I look to where God is
already at work, and gently yet profoundly I push toward his
leading to find the easy yoke and light burden.

I found that when I intentionally set out to practice a discipline, God was ready and willing to provide an opportunity

to learn. I didn't have to search long and far or create huge events. The openings to explore were most always found in the ordinariness of everyday life.

From the brutal wind on the bike and when I voluntarily let my kids guide the day, I learned about the power of submission and the freedom it can bring.

Fasting taught me I can do without and it doesn't have to be bad, even if the deprivation brings up unresolved emotional junk.

The practice of study showed me that I actually do have the ability to learn. And while I may not be very good at memorizing, that doesn't mean the words don't sink in. Whether I'm studying grammar or bass guitar, God is ever happy to be involved in my learning process and redeem that which I thought impossible.

Solitude allowed me to face myself and my emptiness. I learned that boredom can be a wonderful gift and that silence is God's primary language.

From meditation I discovered I didn't need exercise to calm me down; I could find God's stillness at any time and carry it throughout my day.

I got to go around the country offering confessions and found power in naming my wrongs.

With simplicity I faced my bondage to technology and my need to not let others down. I learned that it's not just about what I do but about an inward change that shapes outward behaviors. Even small steps are still steps.

When practicing service, I fooled myself into thinking I was doing something for others and ultimately learned to accept my mix of motives.

I said good-bye to a friend who taught me to use my imagination when I pray. I learned that every breath can be a prayer as I co-labor with God through life.

Guidance brought the call to embrace the desert, and in so doing, I was able to face the suffering of another. Guidance brought me to a place where I could exchange my fear and suffering for connection and freedom.

Worship took me to God's first great book of nature and the awareness that opportunities to respond to God are not confined to church gatherings but ever before me.

I found celebration doesn't have to be a big production but rather can be a general ease about life. Fun and laughter are sacred.

I learned the disciplines are best practiced as a response to God's love and acceptance for who I am. By their very nature, the disciplines reveal our true selves, our motives, and our shortcomings. These are best handled and discovered while sitting in God's tender embrace. Approaching the disciplines without an understanding that we are truly loved is potentially dangerous. This is the path to becoming a Pharisee or immobilized with feelings of never being able to measure up.

I was surprised to discover how the disciplines move and flow into each other. It isn't about twelve rigid practices; in fact, as I go about each day, there are so many simple ways I can intentionally direct my will and actions toward God. While the categories are helpful, they are only constructed to enable us to frame our experiences. In a sense there is only one discipline: an active response to a loving God. It is the process of presenting our will and our lives as a living sacrifice before a good, strong, and caring Father. We learn to respond to the prompting of the Spirit; we hear and obey. This is the call of all Christians. And in the daily little deaths of our actions, in our willingness to suffer, we surely find that something wonderful happens: we are resurrected. We are transformed by God's grace into ordinary saints, people willing and able to respond to life with love, joy, peace, patience, kindness, goodness, faithfulness, gentleness, and self-control.[2] As my dad once said to me, "Spiritual formation is more than just another fad in Western Christianity. It's how we follow Jesus."

I don't feel like the same person who fought the wind on his bike. I have changed. The disciplines have created a significant and helpful learning space from which to navigate life. I feel like the frame in which I view the world is being altered and I'm beginning to understand Jesus's idea of an upside-down kingdom, where the first are last and the last are first,[3] where we favor others over ourselves—not, of course, in an unworthy, low self-esteem manner, but through voluntarily submitting, choosing a life of service rather than selfishness. I find I think of others more than I used to; it's even been instinctual at times. I feel like I'm catching a swift, firm current in life, and things that used to baffle me are starting to come naturally. For instance, I'm not always planning or thinking about the next thing or goal. I'm breathing deeper, enjoying others more. I'm more amazed at beauty and more attuned to the rhythms of love. The goal of practicing the disciplines is to be able to respond to my life as Jesus would if he were me. I'm obviously not there, but I'm moving in the right direction.

I'm learning to let go—that I don't have to control things. So life doesn't work out the way I want. So not all opportunities fall into place. It's okay. I don't have to have my own way. Besides, I'm not very good at knowing how things will turn out, what will be good for me and what won't. I think I know, but my own history tells me otherwise. God loves me. God cares for me. He knows my needs and desires. I can rest in his providence.

I don't fully understand the human process of transformation and the grace God brings from our little actions, but if the disciplines are about freedom, then they've worked. I feel freer than ever before.

Even my time with my family doesn't drain me in the way it used to; in fact, my greatest pleasures seem to come from being with them. I miss them during the day. I no longer look with anticipation toward a trip away. Leaving is painful.

I'm not enslaved to an electronic tether. I don't need to post anything online. I can celebrate without sharing it with the world. I don't need to be successful the way I used to. I don't fear boredom. I don't need to achieve or become. I am free to live, to love, and to be loved. Maybe the greatest and most surprising gift this process has facilitated is that I've become content and grateful with my portion. I'm learning to celebrate in the moment and in the daily routine of life.

I've set some pretty strong boundaries in my life related to rest, silence, and leaving work behind. I'm hardly anxious anymore, and I'm not nearly as moody or cranky as I used to be. I still have moments, but they're much more seldom and they don't last nearly as long. It used to be that I could hold on to hurt or resentment for days. Lately I've found myself able to come to others with a genuine attitude of reconciliation much more quickly, sometimes within minutes.

I'm walking away from this with a new appreciation for stillness and silence, a fascination with fasting from various things, and a new hobby in music.

Ironically, the discipline of study actually led me to the most joy and celebration. I've always loved music, but learning how to play the bass has ignited a passion in me I never knew existed. I'd honestly play all day if I could. I look forward to band practice more than just about any other activity. Who knew that practicing the discipline of study would wind up with me on stage in front of hundreds of people playing bass in a band with my wife? I certainly didn't see that coming! And although playing bass may not seem like a sacred activity, the line between what is spiritual and what is not has all but been erased. I delight in bringing God into new aspects of my life.

I've come back to the picture of the prodigal son, but now I'm thinking about the father. What does it look like to be a person who extends grace to others? What does it mean to wait by the fence for others? To suffer over the loss and brokenness of my brothers and sisters? What does it mean to live a life of loving well?

I'm learning to be like the father. I'm learning to love others well.

Life remains a tangled mess of beauty and suffering, but I like who I'm becoming. I'm learning to be in the present. And while my struggles remain and I'm sure new challenges will present themselves, I feel hopeful for the future in a way I never have before. I don't fear what may come or not come in the same ways I used to. I've found in the simple, mundane moments of my life new opportunities to engage with the awe-filled, wonder-filled, consistently loving, grace-covered presence of God. And it is enough.

When I was growing up, it seemed all stories ended with tidy resolutions. I don't trust happily ever after anymore. But the truth is, my life is really good.

As I walk with my son and daughter down a muddy trail, winter is easing her grip and the subtle signs of spring are hidden around us. I am different. I have changed. Tucked in the corners of life, contentment rests. My midlife angst has come full circle. My longing for more is dying. In its place are hot coffee, card games, family vacations, rock and roll, long walks and restful sleep. The back forty of life will be okay.

I'm okay.

All is well.

All is well.

I awoke this morning with a vision of what would happen if I really gave others the love I feel for them. What if I embraced people and told them the beauty I see in their eyes? Who could I become? Who could we become?

With laughter and hope, we walk.

Joy prevails.

Further Reading

Spiritual Disciplines and Spiritual Formation in General

Athanasius. *Athanasius: The Life of Antony and the Letter to Marcellinus*. Mahwah, NJ: Paulist Press, 1980.

Barton, Ruth Haley. *Sacred Rhythms: Arranging Our Lives for Spiritual Transformation*. Downers Grove, IL: InterVarsity, 2006.

Calhoun, Adele. *Spiritual Disciplines Handbook*. Downers Grove, IL: InterVarsity, 2005.

de Caussade, Jean-Pierre. *Sacrament of the Present Moment*. New York: HarperCollins, 1989.

Foster, Richard J. *Celebration of Discipline*. New York: HarperCollins, 1978.

———. *The Challenge of a Disciplined Life*. New York: HarperCollins, 1985.

———, and James Bryan Smith. *Devotional Classics*. New York: HarperCollins, 1993.

Guyon, Jeanne. *Experiencing the Depth of Jesus Christ*. Sargent, GA: Christian Books Publishing House, 1981.

Kelly, Thomas R. *A Testament of Devotion*. New York: HarperCollins, 1992.

Ortberg, John. *The Life You've Always Wanted: Spiritual Disciplines for Ordinary People*. Grand Rapids: Zondervan, 2002.

Paintner, Christine Valters. *Desert Fathers and Mothers: Early Christian Wisdom Sayings*. Woodstock: Skylight Paths, 2012.

Parham, Richella. *A Spiritual Formation Primer*. Englewood, CO: Renovaré, 2013.

Smith, James Bryan. *The Good and Beautiful God*. Downers Grove, IL: InterVarsity, 2009.

Thomas à Kempis. *Imitation of Christ*. New York: Random House, 1998.

Willard, Dallas. *Spirit of the Disciplines*. New York: HarperCollins, 1988.

———. *Renovation of the Heart*. Colorado Springs: Navpress, 2012.

Submission

DiCamillo, Kate. *The Tiger Rising.* Cambridge: Candlewick Press, 2002.

Hershberger, Guy Franklin. *The Way of the Cross and Human Relations.* Scottsdale: Herald Press, 1958.

King, Martin Luther, Jr. *Strength to Love.* Minneapolis: Fortress Press, 2010.

Fasting

Foster, Richard J. "Fasting." Chap. 4 in *Celebration of Discipline.* New York: HarperCollins, 1978.

Wallis, Arthur. *God's Chosen Fast.* Philadelphia: CLC Publications, 1993.

Study

Adler, Mortimer J., and Charles Van Doren. *How to Read a Book.* New York: Touchstone, 1972.

Kang, Joshua Choonmin. *Scripture by Heart.* Downers Grove, IL: InterVarsity, 2010.

McEntire, Marilyn Chandler. *Caring for Words in a Culture of Lies.* Grand Rapids: Eerdmans, 2009.

Webb, Chris. *The Fire of the Word.* Downers Grove, IL: InterVarsity, 2011.

Solitude

Bill, J. Brent. *Holy Silence.* Brewster, MA: Paraclete Press, 2005.

Nee, Watchman. *Deep Calls Unto Deep.* Anaheim: Living Stream Ministry, 1998.

Nouwen, Henri J. M. *Out of Solitude.* Notre Dame, IN: Ave Maria Press, 2004.

Steere, Douglas. *Together in Solitude.* New York: Crossroad, 1985.

Meditation

Foster, Richard J. *Sanctuary of the Soul.* Downers Grove, IL: InterVarsity, 2011.

Laubach, Frank. *Letters by a Modern Mystic.* Colorado Springs: Purposeful Design Publications 2007.

Lawrence, Brother. *Practicing the Presence of God.* New York: Merchant Books, 2009.

Merton, Thomas. *Spiritual Direction and Meditation.* Collegeville, MN: Liturgical Press, 1960.

Confession

Anderson, Fil. *Running on Empty.* Colorado Springs: Waterbrook Press, 2005.

Buechner, Frederick. *Telling Secrets.* New York: HarperOne, 2000.

Hausherr, Irenee. *Penthos: The Doctrine of Compunction in the Christian East.* Collegeville, MN: Cistercian, 1982.

Simplicity

Eller, Vernard. *The Simple Life: The Christian Stance toward Possessions.* Grand Rapids: Eerdmans, 1973.

Ellul, Jacques. *Money and Power.* Eugene, OR: Wipf & Stock, 2009.

Foster, Richard J. *Freedom of Simplicity*. New York: HarperOne, 2005.

Gish, Arthur. *Beyond the Rat Race*. Eugene, OR: Wipf & Stock, 2002.

Johnson, Jan. *Abundant Simplicity: Discovering the Unhurried Rhythms of Grace*. Downers Grove, IL: InterVarsity, 2011.

Service

Das, Ram, and Paul Gorman. *How Can I Help?* New York: Alfred A. Knopf, 1985.

Nouwen, Henri J. M. *The Genessee Diary*. New York: Image, 1981.

O'Connor, Elizabeth. *Called to Commitment*. New York: Harper & Row, 1963.

Sider, Ronald J. *Rich Christians in an Age of Hunger*. New York: Thomas Nelson, 2005.

Prayer

Foster, Richard J. *Prayer: Finding the Heart's True Home*. New York: HarperOne, 2002.

Griffin, Emilie. *Doors into Prayer: An Invitation*. Brewster, MA: Paraclete Press, 2005.

Hallesby, Ole. *Prayer*. Minneapolis: Augsburg, 1994.

Laubach, Frank. *Letters by a Modern Mystic*. Colorado Springs: Purposeful Design Publications, 2007.

Lawrence, Brother. *The Practice of the Presence of God*. New York: Merchant Books, 2009.

Murray, Andrew. *With Christ in the School of Prayer*. New York: Merchant Books, 2013.

Northumbria Community, The. *Celtic Daily Prayer*. New York: HarperOne, 2002.

Teresa of Avila. *The Interior Castle*. Mahwah, NJ: Paulist Press, 1988.

Guidance

DiCamillo, Kate. *The Miraculous Journey of Edward Tulane*. Cambridge, MA: Candlewick, 2009.

John of the Cross. *Dark Night of the Soul*. Mineola, NY: Dover Publications, 2003.

Singh, Sundar. *At the Master's Feet*. Kissimmee, FL: Signalman Publishing, 2012.

Willard, Dallas. *Hearing God*. Downers Grove, IL: InterVarsity, 2012.

Worship

Muir, John, and Edwin Way Teale. *The Wilderness World of John Muir*. New York: First Mariner Books, 2001.

Peterson, Eugene. *The Pastor*. New York: HarperOne, 2012.

Webber, Robert E. *Ancient-Future Worship: Proclaiming and Enacting God's Narrative*. Grand Rapids: Baker, 2008.

Celebration

Houston, James M. *Joyful Exiles*. Downers Grove, IL: InterVarsity, 2006.

Kirk, Patty. *The Gospel of Christmas: Reflections for Advent*. Downers Grove, IL: InterVarsity, 2012.

Macy, Howard. *Laughing Pilgrims*. Milton Keynes, UK: Paternoster, 2006.

Acknowledgments

Christy Foster, my beautiful bride—You've carried me when I could not walk. You've loved me when I couldn't love myself. You have suffered through my illness and patiently, oh so patiently, you have waited for me to grow into the person you've always known I could be. There is absolutely no way this book would have been completed had you not stepped in and devoted countless hours to editing, guiding, and generally working magic with my jumbled words. You're a living example of much of what I learned in this book, as you seem so naturally content, joyful, and at ease. You not only inspire me but bring special meaning and purpose to my life. Nineteen years, and I like and love you more than ever. You remain my best friend.

Dad—What a gracious gift for you to allow me to enter into your life's work and tinker around. Your support, presence, and friendship mean more to me now than ever before. I will always cherish these memories. Always. Thank you.

Mom—Ever since I was a small child you have seen the challenges and potential that lay before me, and over this you prayed, ached, and suffered. For my entire life you have spoken hopeful and healing words into my uniqueness. Thank you. I've never forgotten or doubted your absolute belief in who I am becoming. Rest easy. All is well.

Autumn Foster—You really inspire me. Not only are you smart and clever, but you're a really good person and fun to be around. I do hope you are able to form your identity around good and positive things. Thanks for your patience while I took time away to write. Thanks for caring about books and words. You are truly beautiful inside and out. I love you and couldn't be prouder to call you my daughter.

Kyren Foster—I've been playing with this project for half of your life, so much of this work belongs to you. It would be amazing to me if one day you leafed through this work and found something helpful in it. That would mean the world to me. You seem to naturally love others so well. Selflessness seems to have already worked its way in. May it stay. I love you. What an honor to be your dad.

My readers—Writing doesn't come easy for me. I've spent many a day working to mental exhaustion only to complete a single page, and sometimes less. It was you and that look in your eye that kept me pecking away, sifting through my jumbled thoughts and ideas, trying desperately to hear your story and mine. On more than one occasion, I've been brought to tears thinking about my gratitude for those who follow my work. You are my community, dispersed and largely unseen, but you help give a certain meaning to my experiences. You give me a place to be known. Thank you for the conversations, emails, and support.

Jason Archer—Few people have the ability to truly rejoice with others when good things happen to them. Thank you for helping me celebrate my life and accomplishments. Thank you for giving me a missional vision of my writing and for reminding me how important honest books are.

David and Naomi Wenger at the Hermitage—Some people step into our lives at fortuitous times. Thank you for giving me space to fall apart. Thank you for stewarding a place for people to learn a new rhythm of life. Your contribution to the kingdom is absolutely profound.

David Wu—For boasting in your weakness. You give me courage to follow.

Mojo—I probably wouldn't have even begun this book had it not been for the enthusiasm and support you offered early on.

Mrs. Mevey and those who committed to weekly prayer for an entire year—Best year of my life.

Kai Nilsen—For Thursdays at 9:30.

Sarah Cunningham—For helping form the vision of what was to come.

Jamin Bradley, Michael Benson, Christy Foster, Shane Pitmon, Ryan Hudson, and all the other people I have played music with as I waded through the writing—Playing was a life-sustaining distraction.

Kimberly Moore-Jumonville—What encouragement your approval has been.

My friends at Renovaré—For believing in this project before you had any reason to.

Bonnie Holiday—Your quiet, often hidden service to others is one of the finest models of the Jesus life I have ever known. Thank you for helping create space for me to write and pursue endeavors outside of the classroom.

Steve Fawver—For your enthusiasm and diligent work on the group guide.

Krista Lingquist—For your clever mind and sharp eyes.

Brittani Browne—For always reminding me to breathe in life. What a spark for life you hold.

Maria Hollister—Your suffering has motivated me to keep writing and teaching.

Caleb Young—For your honest enthusiasm and super cool artwork for the band's EP.

Anne Grizzle—For your life-giving hospitality.

The folks at Baker Books—thanks for your efforts to help this book come into being.

Kate and Stephen Flavin—For your detailed citation efforts.

Robbie Bolton—For the research and writing of the discipline portraits sections.

Acknowledgments

The library staff at Spring Arbor University—For letting me crash in the basement office. You have no idea how much it has meant to have a quiet place to work. I'll get out of your way soon.

The vast majority of this work was written while listening to the The Album Leaf's *Torey's Distraction* and drinking a half-caf Americano.

Notes

Introduction

1. Albert Camus, *The Plague* (New York: McGraw-Hill, 1965), 1.
2. Richard J. Foster, *Celebration of Discipline: The Path to Spiritual Growth* (San Franciso: Harper & Row, 1978).
3. At the present time the languages *Celebration of Discipline* has been translated into include Afrikaans, Amharic, Arabic, Chinese (traditional), Chinese (simplified), Croatian, Czech, Dutch, Farsi, French, German, Hebrew, Indonesian, Japanese, Korean, Lithuanian, Macedonian, Norwegian, Persian, Polish, Portuguese, Romanian, Russian, Spanish, and Turkish.
4. John Paxson quoted in "1993 Finals Overview: Chicago 4, Phoenix 2," NBA Encyclopedia Playoff Edition, accessed August 26, 2013, http://www.nba.com/history/fin9293.html.
5. Malcolm Gladwell, *Outliers: The Story of Success* (New York: Little, Brown, 2008), 393–4.
6. See 1 Timothy 4:7.

Understanding Submission

1. Ephesians 5:21.
2. Mark 8:34.
3. George Matheson, "Make Me a Captive, Lord," in *Sacred Songs* (Edinburgh and London: William Blackwood and Sons, 1890).
4. Philippians 2:7–8.

Chapter 1 Submission

1. John Muir and Linnie Marsh Wolfe, *John of the Mountains: The Unpublished Journals of John Muir* (Boston: Houghton Mifflin, 1938), 439.
2. Matthew 11:30 NIV.

Understanding Fasting

1. See Daniel 1:3–17.
2. See Matthew 4:1–11.
3. See Matthew 6:16–18.

Chapter 2 Fasting

1. Madeleine L'Engle, *A Wrinkle in Time*, 50th ann. commem. ed. (New York: Square Fish, 2012), 81–82.
2. Richard J. Foster, *Sanctuary of the Soul: Journey into Meditative Prayer* (Downers Grove, IL: InterVarsity, 2011), 28.
3. Janet Benge, *Sundar Singh: Footprints over the Mountains* (Seattle, WA: YWAM, 2005), 178.
4. Ibid., 56.

Understanding Study

1. Philippians 4:8.
2. Romans 14:17.

Chapter 3 Study

1. Dallas Willard, *The Great Omission: Reclaiming Jesus' Essential Teachings on Discipleship* (San Francisco: HarperOne, 2006), 189.
2. Joshua Choonmin Kang, *Scripture by Heart: Devotional Practices for Memorizing God's Word* (Downers Grove, IL: InterVarsity, 2010), 15.
3. Romans 12:1 Message.
4. William J. Federer, *George Washington Carver: His Life and Faith in His*

Own Words (St. Louis, MO: Amerisearch, 2002), 36.

Interlude: Discipline Hazard #1: The Self-Hatred Narrative

1. Dallas Willard, Twitter post, July 20, 2013, 4:53 p.m., https://twitter.com/Dallas AWillard/status/358736518107512832.
2. Jean Pierre de Caussaude, quoted in "Quotes from Fr Jean Pierre de Caussade, a French Jesuit Priest (1675–1751)," Sozein, 2014, http://sozein.org.uk/de%20 Caussade.htm.
3. Julian of Norwich, quoted in Elizabeth Spearing, *Medieval Writings on Female Spirituality* (New York: Penguin, 2002), 206.

Understanding Solitude

1. Thomas Merton, *Through the Year with Thomas Merton: Daily Meditations from His Writings*, ed. Thomas P. McDonnell, February 4, "In Deep Solitude" (Garden City, NY: Image Books, 1985), 22.

Chapter 4 Solitude

1. Stanley Kunitz, *Passing Through: The Later Poems, New and Selected* (New York: W.W. Norton, 1995), 68.
2. Ecclesiastes 1:14 NIV.
3. Anthony of the Desert quoted in Sister Benedicta Ward, *Selections from the Sayings of the Desert Fathers* (Kalamazoo, MI: Cistercian Publications, 1975), 8.

Understanding Meditation

1. Isaiah 55:3.
2. Quoted in Foster, *Sanctuary of the Soul*, 78.
3. Catherine de Hueck Doherty quoted in Gerard Thomas Straub, *The Sun and Moon over Assisi: A Personal Encounter with Francis and Clare* (Cincinnati, OH: St. Anthony Messenger Press, 2000), 508.
4. Ephesians 2:21–22.

Chapter 5 Meditation

1. Meister Eckhart quoted in Martin Manser, *The Westminster Collection of Christian Quotes* (Louisville: Westminster John Knox Press, 2001), 306.
2. Reinhold Niebuhr, "The Serenity Prayer" (1953), quoted in Judy Bauer, *The Essential Catholic Prayer Book: A Collection of Private and Community Prayers* (St. Louis: Liguori Publications, 1999), 24.
3. Martin Luther King Jr., "Where Do We Go from Here?" speech, Atlanta, GA, August 16, 1967, text available online at http://mlk-kpp01.stanford.edu/index.php/encyclopedia/documentsentry/where_do_we_go_from_here_delivered_at_the_11th_annual_sclc_convention/.
4. Psalm 46:10 NIV.
5. 1 Kings 19:12 KJV.
6. Henri Nouwen, *The Way of the Heart* (Toronto: Ballantine, 1981), 52.

Understanding Confession

1. 2 Corinthians 5:21.
2. 1 John 1:9.
3. Bernard of Clairvaux, "Of Him Who Did Salvation Bring" (hymn), as quoted in Martin Madan, *A Collection of Psalms and Hymns Extracted from Various Authors*, 1760, http://cyberhymnal.org/htm/o/h/ohwdisab.htm.

Chapter 6 Confession

1. Bill Wilson and Robert Smith, *Alcoholics Anonymous* (New York: Alcoholics Anonymous World Service, 1939).
2. "The Twelve Steps of Alcoholics Anonymous," Alcoholics Anonymous General Service Office, 2002, http://www.aa.org/en_pdfs/smf-121_en.pdf.
3. Ibid.
4. Nathan Foster, *Wisdom Chaser: Finding My Father at 14,000 Feet* (Downers Grove, IL: InterVarsity, 2010).
5. Exodus 3:14 NIV.
6. John Michael Talbot, "Hiding Place," on *Hiding Place*, Sparrow 1193, 1989, cassette.
7. See Philippians 4:8.

Understanding Simplicity

1. See Matthew 6:33.
2. Dietrich Bonhoeffer, *Ethics* (New York: Touchstone, 1995), 70.

Chapter 7 Simplicity

1. Blaise Pascal, *Pensées*, trans. W. F. Trotter (New York: E. P. Dutton, 1958), 39.
2. See Philippians 4:12.
3. See Matthew 6:33.

4. Thomas Kelly, *A Testament of Devotion* (New York: Harper, 1941), 3.

5. Julian of Norwich, *Revelations of Divine Love*, trans. Grace Warrack, Christian Classics Ethereal Library, updated March 27, 2013, http://www.ccel.org/ccel/julian/revelations.

6. Dallas Willard, *The Divine Conspiracy: Rediscovering Our Hidden Life in God* (New York: HarperCollins, 1998).

7. Matthew 23:27.

8. See Galatians 5:22–23.

Understanding Service

1. John 13:12–15.

2. Matthew 12:20.

3. William Law, *A Serious Call to a Devout and Holy Life*, Christian Classics Ethereal Library, http://www.ccel.org/browse/bookInfo?id=law/serious_call.

Chapter 8 Service

1. Richard J. Foster, *Celebration of Discipline: The Path to Spiritual Growth*, 20th ann. ed. (San Francisco: HarperSanFrancisco, 1998), 130.

2. See Matthew 20:16.

3. Foster, *Celebration of Discipline*, 128.

4. See Luke 7:38.

Interlude: Discipline Hazard #2: My Inner Pharisee

1. George Fox quoted in J. Brent Bill, *Holy Silence: The Gift of Quaker Spirituality* (Brewster, MA: Paraclete Press, 2005), 26.

2. Ibid., 99.

3. Matthew 7:2 NIV.

4. See Matthew 7:3.

5. See Luke 15:11–32.

6. See Matthew 23:15.

7. This idea comes from Dallas Willard, *The Divine Conspiracy*, 283.

8. See John 13:35.

Understanding Prayer

1. C. S. Lewis, *Mere Christianity* (1952; New York: HarperCollins, 2001), 205–6.

2. Augustine quoted in Richard J. Foster, *Prayer: Finding the Heart's True Home* (New York: HarperCollins, 1992), 255.

3. Denise Nowakowski Baker, *Julian of Norwich's Showings: From Vision to Book* (Princeton: Princeton University Press, 1997), 145.

4. Charles Wesley, "Jesus, Lover of My Soul," 1740.

Chapter 9 Prayer

1. Quoted in M. V. Kamath, *Gandhi: A Spiritual Journey* (Mumbai: Indus Source, 2007), 70.

2. 1 Thessalonians 5:17.

3. Thomas Merton, *Contemplative Prayer* (New York: Random House, 2009), 13.

4. See Luke 8:46.

5. Teresa of Avila, *The Life of Saint Teresa of Avila by Herself* (New York: Penguin, 1957), 44.

6. Ibid., 71.

7. Ibid., 93.

8. Ibid., 409.

Understanding Guidance

1. E. Stanley Jones, *A Song of Ascents* (Nashville: Abingdon, 1979), 190.

2. Proverbs 11:3.

3. Psalm 119:105.

4. See John 10:14.

Chapter 10 Guidance

1. See 1 Timothy 4:7.

2. 1 Timothy 4:7.

3. Henri Nouwen, *The Way of the Heart: The Spirituality of the Desert Fathers and Mothers* (New York: HarperCollins, 1981), 54.

4. Matthew 27:46.

5. 1 Thessalonians 5:17.

Understanding Worship

1. Isaiah 6:3, 5.

2. Revelation 1:10.

3. Revelation 1:17.

4. George Fox, "CCLXXXVIII: To Friends in Carolina," *A Collection of Many Select and Christian Epistles, Letters and Testimonies, Written on Sundry Occasions, by That Ancient, Eminent, Faithful Friend and Minister of Christ Jesus, George Fox*, vol. 8 of *The Works of George Fox* (Philadelphia: Marcus T. C. Gould, 1831), 37.

5. Colossians 3:16.

Chapter 11 Worship

1. Foster, *Celebration of Discipline*, 158.

2. Thomas Kelly, "The Gathered Meeting," Tract Association of Friends, http://www.tractassociation.org/tracts/the-gathered-meeting/.

3. John Muir, *My First Summer in the Sierra* (Boston: Houghton Mifflin, 1911), 196.

Understanding Celebration

1. Saint Augustine quoted in Eugene H. Peterson, *God's Message for Each Day: Wisdom from the Word of God* (Nashville: Thomas Nelson, 2004), 227.

2. Galatians 5:22–23.

3. Nehemiah 8:10.

Chapter 12 Celebration

1. Léon Bloy, *Letters to His Fiancée* (London: Sheed and Ward, 1937), 57.

2. Lewis, *Mere Christianity*, 136–37.

3. Foster, *Celebration of Discipline*, 191.

4. St. Francis of Assisi, *Francis and Clare: The Complete Works* (Mahwah, NJ: Paulist Press 1982), 123.

Conclusion

1. Norwich, *Revelations of Divine Love.*

2. See Galatians 5:22–23.

3. See Matthew 20:16.

Nathan Foster is an associate professor of social work and theology at Spring Arbor University, where he holds the Andrews Chair in Spiritual Formation. He is director of teaching ministries for Renovaré as well as a licensed clinical social worker, certified addictions counselor, public speaker, bassist for Christy & The Professors, and the author of *Wisdom Chaser: Finding My Father at 14,000 Feet*. He currently resides in Michigan with his wife and two children. To connect with Nathan or book speaking engagements, visit www.nathanfosterprojects.com.